My Father:

JOSEPH CONRAD

My Father:
JOSEPH CONRAD

by BORYS CONRAD

Coward-McCann, Inc., New York

Permission to quote from a letter by John Galsworthy has kindly been given by the John Galsworthy Estate.
Permission to quote from Joseph Conrad's correspondence with Richard Curle and Sir Sydney Colvin and a short extract from *The Shadow Line* has kindly been given by J. M. Dent & Sons Ltd., London, publishers of the Collected Edition of Joseph Conrad's work, and the Trustees of the Joseph Conrad Estate.

TO M.R.R.

Illustrations follow page 160

My Father:
JOSEPH CONRAD

Prologue

THE INCIDENTS recorded within these pages are described exactly as I remember them and date from the time when my parents took over the tenancy of Pent Farm from Ford Madox Hueffer at the end of 1898.

Their previous home was at Ivy Walls Farm in Stanford-le-Hope, Essex, and it was there that I was born on January 15th of the same year, so that I was still too young when we moved to Pent Farm to retain any memories of my birthplace, although its outward appearance later became familiar to me as a result of having it pointed out by my Mother when we passed it, from time to time, on our way to visit Father's oldest English friend, G. F. W. Hope and his family, who lived in the same village.

I imagine that the expense of my arrival into the world and our subsequent removal to Pent Farm was just about covered by the money received for the *Nigger of the Narcissus* which was published about that time; but I may be wrong: what knowledge I have of my Father's literary activities has been acquired later – very much later – in my life and is not necessarily strictly accurate.

For me, life began at Pent Farm and the very first thing I was taught – as soon as I was capable of learning anything at all – was that I must not, under any circumstances, intrude into my Father's room, or create any unseemly noise or

11

disturbance within earshot of it, when he was 'doing his writing'. At that time this phrase was, to me, synonymous with the scribblings in my picture books made with the aid of coloured crayons, and I suspect I was a little puzzled as to why my Father should demand absolute peace and quiet for his activities while I had to carry out mine squatting on the floor, under the kitchen table or even outside on the garden path. However, this initial lesson was quickly learned.

It never occurred to me to disobey my parents, and I do not remember ever being punished by either of them. My Father's method of rebuke was to screw his monocle firmly in his eye and assume an expression of truly diabolical savagery. This performance was at times supplemented by shaking his forefinger at me. My Mother achieved the same result with far less effort – by merely looking at me, without any noticeable change of expression, and saying 'No, dear' or 'You must not do that, dear' in the gentle tone of voice which was characteristic of her.

She was the ideal wife for Joseph Conrad: with her rigid self-control she was impervious to his emotional outbursts which, although alarming to those who did not know him well, were always of brief duration – except when he was goaded by the pain of an attack of gout – and, more often than not, followed by a shout of laughter.

I believe, in spite of anything some of his many literary biographers may have said, that his best writing was done at Pent Farm. After all, *Youth*, *The Heart of Darkness*, *Lord Jim*, *Tales of Unrest*, *Nostromo*, *Typhoon*, *The Secret Agent* and *Chance* belong, among others, to the Pent Farm period, and most of them were typed by my Mother upon a monolithic typewriter called a Yost, which possessed an irresistible fascination for me. Its sheer bulk and weight – my Mother was unable to lift it off the table without help – in contrast to its eventual successor – one of the earliest portables, a Blick – was quite astonishing.

I had no nurse or other attendant as a child and was allowed to 'run wild' about the farm. My Mother was already too physically handicapped to keep up with me and my Father, whenever he emerged from his literary lair, was far more likely to encourage me in any mischief I had in hand, than to impose any restraint. My only occasional companions anywhere near my own age were my youngest uncle and my youngest aunt – both being only a few years older than myself. My Mother, the second in a family of nine, had four brothers and four sisters but it was only the three younger ones who were involved to any extent in our family life. Ethel, the eldest of this trio, acted from time to time as voluntary, unpaid, governess to her youngest brother my Uncle Frank, her young sister Nellie, and myself. She was also the only member of my Mother's family of whom my Father was really fond, with the exception of my maternal Great Aunt – Miss Sex – a handsome old lady of imposing presence, whose warmth and charm of manner captivated everyone who came in contact with her, including my Father. She was highly intelligent and a brilliant conversationalist; and I believe she was the only person entirely unconnected with the literary world who was ever invited to join in those long and animated discussions behind the closed door of his room, which often lasted till the small hours of the morning. I was devoted to my Great Aunt Alice whereas, I must confess, I had no affection whatever for her sister – my Grandmother – a grim-featured old lady who habitually wore an expression of disgust and disapproval which seemed to me to be entirely in keeping with her character.

After the birth of my brother in 1906 it became obvious that my Mother would no longer be able to devote sufficient time to the typing of my Father's manuscripts and moreover his recurring attacks of gout often affected his hands, making it difficult and painful to write, so it was decided to engage a secretary. Little or no mention has been made in the various biographies of my Father of the lady who, after several unsatisfactory candidates, eventually occupied this post. She was a tall willowy female, then I think, about thirty, with a supercilious manner and a somewhat vacant expression. She also had very thick long brown hair which she wore in an insecurely anchored bun on the nape of her long neck, which used to wobble about as she moved, in a most intriguing manner and finally disintegrate, leaving her hair free to cascade over her shoulders – usually at the most inappropriate and embarrassing moments.

Nevertheless she retained her position in our household – spasmodically until the time of my Father's death. She would be with us for weeks or even months, and then depart perhaps for a long period, until recalled – usually by telegram – to resume her duties. Her name was Miss M. Hallowes and the fact that my Father not only tolerated her presence in the house but even developed some affection for her, was due, I believe, solely to the facts that she was a good typist and possessed the ability to sit quite silent and motionless in front of her machine, hands resting tranquilly in her lap, for long periods, reacting promptly to a word, a phrase, or a sudden outburst of continuous speech, hurled at her abruptly as he prowled about the room or sat hunched up in his big armchair, as he dictated directly onto the typewriter.

He always worked in complete seclusion and no one except my Mother was permitted to intrude upon this privacy. Nor did he discuss his work or the origin of his stories among the family. Any discussion of his own work or that of his friends always took place behind the closed door of his room, and usually late at night.

The opening pages of this book deal with the early part of the year 1900, when I was little more than two years old, so that the recollections of my Father's intimate friends at that time are inevitably somewhat incomplete; except for John Galsworthy, who remains as vividly in my memory of that time as do my parents. It was to him that I wrote my first letter – I suspect with some little assistance from my Mother. It arose from the fact that we had been staying with him for a few days at his home in London and is commendably brief:

Dear Mr. Jack,

I want to tell you how much I did like to stay in your flat. Thank you ever so much. I am writing this letter all myself.

Borys.

I conclude this prologue by quoting – in part – Galsworthy's own account of his first meeting with Joseph Conrad, and I do so because it is completely in accord with my own memories of the man who was my Father.

' ... It was in March 1893 that I first met Conrad on board the English sailing-ship *Torrens* in Adelaide Harbour. He was superintending the stowage of cargo. Very dark he looked in the burning sunlight – tanned, with a peaked brown beard, almost black hair, and dark brown eyes, over which the lids were deeply folded. He was thin, not tall,

15

his arms very long, his shoulders broad, his head set rather forward. He spoke to me with a strong foreign accent. He seemed to me strange on an English ship. For fifty-six days I sailed in his company.

'The chief mate bears the main burden of a sailing ship. All the first night he was fighting a fire in the hold. None of us seventeen passengers knew of it till long after. It was he who had most truck with the tail of that hurricane off the Leeuwin, and later with another storm. He was a good seaman, watchful of the weather, quick in handling the ship; considerate with the apprentices – we had a long unhappy Belgian youth among them, who took unhandily to the sea and dreaded going aloft; Conrad compassionately spared him all he could. With the crew he was popular; they were individuals to him, not a mere gang; and long after he would talk of this or that among them, especially of old Andy the sailmaker: "I liked that old fellow, you know." He was friendly with the second mate, a cheerful, capable young seaman, very English; and respectful, if faintly ironic, to his whiskered, stout old English captain. I, supposed to be studying navigation for the Admiralty Bar, would every day work out the position of the ship with the captain. On one side of the saloon table we would sit and check our observations with those of Conrad, who from the other side of the table would look at us a little quizzically. For Conrad had commanded ships, and his subordinate position on the *Torrens* was only due to the fact that he was still then convalescent from the Congo experience which had nearly killed him. Many evening watches in fine weather we spent on the poop. Ever the great teller of a tale, he had already nearly twenty years of tales to tell. Tales of ships and storms, of Polish revolution, of his youthful Carlist gun-running adventure, of the Malay seas, and the Congo; and of men and men; all to a listener who had the insatiability of a twenty-five-year-old.

'On that ship he talked of life, not literature; and it is NOT true that I introduced him to the life of letters. At Cape Town, on my last evening, he asked me to his cabin, and I remember feeling that he outweighed for me all the other experiences of that voyage. Fascination was Conrad's great characteristic – the fascination of vivid expressiveness and zest, of his deeply affectionate heart, and his far-ranging subtle mind . . .

'I used to stay with him a good deal from 1895–1905, first at Stanford in Essex and then at Stanford in Kent. He was indefatigably good to me while my own puppy eyes were opening to literature, and I was still in the early stages of that struggle with his craft which a writer worth his salt never quite abandons.

'His affectionate interest was always wholly generous. In his letters to me – two to three hundred – there is not a sentence which breaks, or even jars, the feeling that he cared that one should do good work. There is some valuable criticism, but never any impatience, and no stinting of appreciation or encouragement. He never went back on friendship. The word "loyalty" has been much used by those who write or speak of him. It has been well used. He was always loyal to what he had at heart – to his philosophy, to his work, and to his friends; he was loyal even to his dislikes (not few) and to his scorn.'

Chapter One

IN THE MEMORIES which I retain of my early childhood my
Father appears clearly as the central figure around whom our
family life revolved, whereas my Mother's image is far less
distinct. In fact the clearest recollection I have of her from
that period, is of a quiet person who moved around slowly
in the oak-beamed kitchen of Pent Farm as she prepared our
meals, and who was invariably at hand in time of crisis –
such as ministering to my Father during his periodical attacks
of gout and tending my frequent cuts and bruises with calm
efficiency. Complete imperturbability and apparent lack of
emotion under any circumstances, in spite of almost constant
pain and physical discomfort, remained with her throughout
her life. This unassailable placidity was almost frightening
at times.

I was an only child for the first nine years of my life and,
in the isolation of the Pent, I lived mainly in an adult world;
even the knife and boot boy, thirteen or fourteen years of age,
fell into this category from my point of view. Whenever my
Father was busy with his writing, I sought the company of
this boy and the gardener, and of those who worked on the
farm.

My interest in all things mechanical began at a very early
age so that, with my Father's encouragement and occasional
help, together with the assistance of the gardener and the
boy, a strange object came into being. It was supposed to be

a motor car but, in truth, the only similarity between this contraption and the cars of the period lay in the fact that it possessed a wheel at each corner and some method of steering. In its original form it was guided approximately in the desired direction with the aid of two pieces of rope which my Father cut surreptitiously from Mother's clothes line! As our technique improved, modifications were incorporated and it eventually developed a steering wheel. The problem of motive power was, however, beyond us at this time but was eventually solved by another raid upon Mother's clothes line from which he returned in triumph, with the clothes prop, the forked end of which he applied to the rear of the contraption upon which I was already seated. Then he laboriously pushed it up out of the hollow where our home was situated, and along the lane which rose in a series of three short slopes with a brief downward dip between each one. Arriving at the highest point, he helped me turn it round and, giving me an encouraging pat on the back said: 'Off you go Boy,' and sent me on my way. Fortunately for my safety, the dips between each slope checked my speed sufficiently and I arrived at the bottom intact, and with sufficient momentum remaining to carry me right home. This adventure became a regular part of our routine and the contraption was eventually fitted with a crude braking system for emergencies. It was, perhaps, fortunate there was little or no traffic on the roads in those days, particularly as the braking system only operated on one wheel!

One day, a wondrous vehicle materialized, which not only vaguely resembled a motor car, but also possessed motive power in the shape of bicycle pedals. My Father had this machine constructed in secret by the village wheel-wright and produced it as a surprise for my birthday. Unhappily it was so heavy and cumbersome that I was quite unable to get it under way with the pedals, and we had to supplement the motive power with the clothes prop. His disappointment was almost as great as my own, but I was soon able to apply pressure to the pedals more efficiently and was thus able to manoeuvre the machine well enough on level ground. The clothes prop had, however, to be called into service for our expeditions up the lane.

When I visited Pent Farm recently I was surprised to see how little it had changed in appearance; and the room in which my Father used to work looked astonishingly familiar. There was an oak table in the corner in the same position as I remembered his desk, and an armchair by the fire exactly as his huge wingchair had been placed. This chair, which remains in my memory as the focal point of the scenery upon the stage of our family life, invariably presented its back to the door so that, when in use, the occupant was invisible to anyone entering the room. Invisible, that is, with the exception of one foot which protruded at the side, owing to his invariable habit of sitting with his knees crossed. I believe we could all assess the mood of the head of the house by a surreptitious glance at that foot. If it was motionless it could be safely assumed that its owner was reading or thinking, and in a reasonably tranquil frame of mind, but any movement of the limb indicated that all was not well. In fact, the degree of his displeasure could be fairly accurately gauged by the rapidity with which the foot waggled, and really violent movement was a danger signal unwise to ignore.

The table, in the position once occupied by his desk, seemed to be somewhat bare until I realized this was due to the absence of the big paraffin lamp, which had stood on the corner of the desk in those days, and provided the sole illumination in the room. Then I remembered an occasion when, as a very small boy, I was awakened by my Mother in the middle of the night, and carried downstairs and into the garden, through clouds of evil-smelling smoke. Having thrust me into the arms of someone whose identity I do not recollect, she returned to the house and assisted my Father in smothering the flames which were visible through the window of his room. It was not until many years later that I was able to appreciate the magnitude of the disaster which occurred that night. He had been working on the concluding chapters of a story, the first part of which had already gone to the printers for serial publication, when the glass bowl of the lamp burst; the ensuing conflagration completely destroying the manuscript which was already overdue for despatch. When I grew old enough to realize the immense effort his creative genius demanded of him I was able to understand in some degree, the agonies through which he must have passed while re-writing those lost chapters against the clock.

I have no direct knowledge as to which of his stories was involved, nor have I found any previous reference to this catastrophe in print. My own personal view is that it was one of the stories in *Typhoon* – possibly *Anny Foster* – which first appeared in the *Illustrated London News*, in December, 1901; but *Falk* and *The End of the Tether* also belong to the same period.

The huge tythe barn, reputed to be one of the finest in the country, was destroyed by fire some years ago and the granary, perched upon its four stone pedestals, as a protection against the depredations of rats, has recently disintegrated; but the wagon-shed remains, and also the coach-house where our carriage was kept.

The ancient chestnut tree still spreads its venerable shade over the garden and, as I stood beneath it, I remembered an occasion when some visitors were being entertained there to a picnic tea. During this festivity my Father conceived the idea of fixing a swing on one of the branches for my amusement. He decided to carry out this operation at once, and I have a very clear recollection of the crack of the breaking branch and his abrupt descent among the guests and the tea-cups: also of his loud exclamations of alarm and annoyance.

During the early years of my life he would often remain at his desk writing till far into the night and sometimes he would rise in the small hours of the morning, don his dressing-gown and return to his labours. I learned of this because I slept in the dressing-room which opened from my parents' bedroom, and I was often drowsily aware of his presence when he crept in, either to remove his dressing-gown or to put it on. Sometimes I would waken up sufficiently to observe him as he bent over my bed to look at me. If I showed any awareness of this an admonitory finger was shaken over my head.

He used to sleep at odd times during the day, in his wing-chair – as I discovered from my ability, at a very early age, to climb the grape-vine which grew up the wall of the Pent, and peep at him through the window. If he caught me in the act he would either treat me to a glare and a shake of the admonitory finger, or come out and join me in the garden. I believe he then still retained the habit of having four-hourly periods of rest as a result of his watch-keeping at sea. However this may be, I certainly benefited from the routine because it enabled him to devote a considerable part of the day to playing with me and inventing new games for my entertainment;

23

even upon occasion, aiding and abetting me in some minor act of mischief. The latter I remember, did not always meet with entire approval from my Mother.

As I stood at that familiar room in the Pent, talking to the present owner, the memories came flooding back: of our horse and dog-cart and the odd adventures which befell us upon the weekly journeys to Hythe to do the household shopping; of the activities on and around the farm, and of the ageing brothers Finn who worked it. Bearded men – one dark the other grizzled – known to me as 'Brown Finn and Grey Finn', of the admiration with which my Father and I watched these two sturdy countrymen at harvest time as they scythed a way round the verge of the cornfield to provide space for the horse-drawn combine reaper to start operations. The rhythmical swing of those bowed shoulders went on, as it seemed interminably, without a falter or even a brief pause for rest. If we happened to be in the field at noon when they stopped for refreshment, I remember noting the unfailing courtesy with which these men accepted my Father's offer of cigarettes which they then carefully dismembered with their knarled fingers prior to cramming the tobacco into their blackened fragments of clay pipe which they smoked with apparent enjoyment. When I grew older I discovered they would have infinitely preferred to smoke the strong black shag obtainable in the village shop, but they were far too well-mannered to risk offending him by refusing his cigarettes. They also consumed an incredible quantity of cold tea, without milk or sugar, which they brought with them in bottles. Brown Finn once persuaded me to sample this beverage; an experiment which disgusted me to such an extent that I decided to deprive him of my company for several days, and resulted in my receiving the quite unnecessary advice from my Father to 'have nothing more to do with that damned concoction'.

As I left the Pent on that day and drove homeward over the hills within the folds of which the house lies, still more memories returned and I found myself talking to my companion about my first air-gun presented to me when I was barely six years old and of my Father's very strict instruction in the care and handling of fire-arms. I recalled my expeditions upon those hillsides with my gun and my dog in an exciting, but mainly fruitless, pursuit of rabbits. Great and solitary adventures shared only, as I then thought, with my faithful hound and it was a long time before I realized I had been under my Father's almost constant observation by virtue of his binoculars. Later in life I greatly appreciated his wisdom in concealing the fact of this supervision from me. It must have helped to give me confidence, and anyway I would have been bitterly disappointed had my illusion of solitary adventure been shattered.

It was this and many other incidents of a like nature that helped to develop the very close and affectionate companionship which came to exist between us, the memory of which I shall treasure to the end of my days. He possessed a gun of his own at that time. It was, to me, an awe-inspiring weapon known as a rook rifle, and with it, he was in the habit of, to use his own expression, bombarding the rats as they scrambled about on the thatched roof of the old tythe barn. Although he was a pretty good marksman, they were a difficult moving target and I cannot recollect him having any great success.

I do, however, remember one occasion when the weapon came near to being brought into use in what he imagined to be the defence of his home and family. This event involved

25

my maternal Grandmother with whom he was not upon the best of terms. In fact they detested one another and this must, I believe, have been almost the last time she entered our home until the time of his death. I have no recollection of the reason for her presence on this occasion and it is, in any case, unimportant; but it would appear she must have suffered some sort of digestive upset in the small hours of the night which necessitated rising from her bed.

The toilet facilities at the Pent were housed in a separate building of considerable size; having been designed by the architect, if any, upon what one might describe as social and family lines inasmuch as it provided adult accommodation for two and, at an appropriately lower level, juvenile accommodation for one. It also possessed a heavy oak door fitted with two iron hasps through which the occupant, or occupants, were supposed to pass a piece of wood, thus forming a crude bolt. It was towards this building that Grandmama directed her steps, but her movements attracted my Father's attention as he sat writing at his desk. He immediately seized his rifle and rushed out of the front door at about the same moment as Grandmama emerged from the back entrance. Seeing no sign of an intruder, he proceeded to make a reconnaissance. Grandmama must, in her turn, have heard the noise of his approach and fled, with the result that they would appear to have made one or more circuits of the house before Grandmama recovered her wits sufficiently to run for shelter in the toilet building. Unfortuately, she omitted to make use of the wooden bolt and my Father, having as he thought, run the intruder to earth, burst into the building shouting: 'Come out you – Damn you.'

What actually happened within those walls before the moment of mutual recognition, I am unable to record since, to my great regret, I was not among those present. I suspect, however, that this unhappy contretemps must have put the final seal upon the antipathy which already existed between them; this is all the more likely from the fact that he was then writing *Nostromo* which must have imposed a great strain upon him as is confirmed by his own words:

'It took the best part of the years 1903/4 to do; with many intervals of renewed hesitation, lest I should lose myself in the ever-enlarging vistas opening before me as I progressed deeper in my knowledge of the country. Often also, when I had thought myself to a standstill over the tangled affairs of the republic, I would, figuratively speaking, pack my bag, rush away from Sulaco for a change of air and write a few pages of *The Mirror of the Sea*. But generally, as I have said before, my sojourn on the continent of Latin America, famed for its hospitality, lasted for about two years. On my return I found (speaking somewhat in the style of Captain Gulliver) my family all well, my wife heartily glad to learn that the fuss was all over, and our small boy considerably grown during my absence.'

From this I think it may be safely deduced that the necessity of making, as it were, a special brief return from Latin America for the sole purpose of chasing his mother-in-law around the house with a loaded rifle must have infuriated him.

Our weekly shopping expeditions to Hythe always afforded me great enjoyment. Usually my Father harnessed the mare himself but there were times when he would tell me to: 'Go and find Grey Finn and ask him please to harness the mare and "put her to".' The latter instruction meaning, in the local language, to attach the mare to the dog-cart. I would dash off in search of my good friend and stay with him supervising the operation until it was completed and then report to my Father. First I was hoisted into the small rear seat and strapped firmly into position, then my Mother climbed laboriously into the front seat using the hub of the wheel as a step. Finally my Father mounted to the box seat, attired in his havelock – a long garment, half cloak and half overcoat – and with bowler hat and monocle firmly in position. He then took up reins and whip; Grey Finn let go the mare's head and stepped back raising a finger to his dilapidated canvas hat in respectful farewell, and the expedition was under way. The road to Hythe, along winding and hilly lanes, was about six miles and, therefore, it was nearly an hour later when we turned in under the archway leading to the stable-yard of the White Hart Inn. The ostler came forward with the usual respectful and friendly greeting, to unharness the mare and my parents having released me from the rear seat, we entered the Inn by the back door to be greeted by its proprietress, Miss Cobay, a large and majestic female with the most improbable yellow hair. My Father either established himself in the bar-parlour and conversed with the locals or walked across the road to the antique shop where he would browse around happily and discuss the various exhibits with Mr. Ninnes, the proprietor, while my Mother and I attended to the shopping. Our business completed, we returned to the Inn for lunch with Miss Cobay, in her own private parlour. Then the ostler would lead forth our chariot, heave me up into my seat to be strapped in, and the homeward journey began.

Upon one of these journeys the mare stumbled and fell heavily with the result that my Father suddenly became airborne and, to my alarm and astonishment sailed through the air in a crouching posture like some huge frog, and came to rest seated squarely upon the mare's head. My Mother, being much heavier, merely toppled over the splash board and landed upon the animal's hind quarters: a most dangerous and unenviable position. Thanks to my safety strap, I remained in my seat and thus had an excellent grandstand view which probably accounts for the very clear recollection I have of the event.

It was upon this occasion I first became aware of my Father's complete composure and competence when confronted with a real emergency. He had immediately realized my Mother's dangerous situation and, instead of going to her assistance, remained firmly seated upon the animal's head and called out to her, 'Scramble away from her legs, Jess, she can't kick you while I remain here.' As soon as my Mother had carried out his instructions he rose, got the mare up onto her feet and calmed her down. Then he helped my Mother back to her seat and we proceeded slowly home in complete silence. He merely glanced at me; probably to see if I was unduly frightened, but said nothing at all until we were once more inside the Pent. Then: 'Any damage Jess, dear?' and upon being reassured on this point he instructed me to: 'Go and find Grey Finn, Boy, and ask him to come and help me to dress the mare's knees.'

Chapter Two

THERE WERE a number of visitors to the Pent in those early days, some of whom I remember clearly, but there were others whose images have become very blurred.

Edward Garnett for instance, whom I remember only as an ungainly and shaggy figure shambling across the fields from the station. The Ford Madox Hueffer of those days is equally shadowy although he must have been a frequent visitor while collaborating with my Father and, moreover, was the previous tenant of the Pent, and actually loaned us the house together with some of his furniture for a period until we took over the tenancy. I got to know Ford better in later years and we were together for a time in France during the First World War. Most vividly I remember John Galsworthy – Uncle Jack to me – whom I would run to meet as he strode along the field path from the station. At that time he affected a monocle which he wore without any safety cord or ribbon, and kept in his waistcoat pocket when not in use. It was his habit to entertain me by screwing the lens firmly into his eye and then raising his eyebrow, thus allowing it to fall until he caught it at waist level and restored it to his pocket. This performance afforded me great pleasure but I appreciated even more that of our young domestic servant who, entering the room on one occasion while the act was in progress, uttered a startled exclamation and dived forward in an attempt to rescue the falling disc with the result that she butted Uncle Jack soundly in the midriff with her head. He took it in good part and to my relief, did not abandon the entertainment as a result of this contretemps.

One event which remains very clear in my memory is the occasion of H. G. Wells' first visit to luncheon, a meal over which my Mother, who always coped personally with all culinary matters, had taken particular pains. To begin with H.G. arrived half-an-hour late. This fact, in itself, was sufficient to ruffle my Father's temper and disrupt my Mother's preparations for the repast, but it faded into insignificance when H.G. took his place at the table and announced his wish to lunch off a glass of milk and two aspirins from his waistcoat pocket. So far as I recollect, my Mother's self-control was quite admirable, but my Father, having first screwed his monocle firmly in position, treated the guest to a most virulent glare. I have no further recollection of this visit but it must have ended upon a friendly note because we went to the Wells' home, Spade House, upon several subsequent occasions. It was perched upon the cliffs at Sandgate and, as the house was only about two miles from Hythe, we would sometimes vary our weekly shopping routine and, after lunching with Miss Cobay, continue along the coast to Sandgate to take tea with the Wells family. I think I must have found these visits very boring because they seem to have left no impression upon my memory.

I have, however, a very clear recollection of our occasional visits to Henry James. He lived in Rye which lies some fourteen miles from the Pent, and it was, therefore, quite a considerable journey. The house was situated only a few yards from the still famous Mermaid Inn, and it was here we left the mare and dog-cart in the care of the ostler. Apparently Henry James was very fond of me but I found his method of demonstrating this affection rather irksome. It was his habit to lift me up onto his knees and pass an arm around my middle while he carried on a most animated conversation with my Father. Sometimes, when absorbed by the subject under discussion or in the heat of a friendly argument, he would squeeze me with such violence as to cause me some distress. My Mother always kept a close eye upon me on these occasions and, when she saw I had had all I could take, would come forward and tactfully rescue me from the great man's clutches.

There was one friend in particular whose occasional visits always delighted me – William Rothenstein who, within a few minutes of his arrival, would be squatting on the floor with my box of paints producing the most charming water-colour sketches of my many mechanical toys and of myself operating them. In later years I had several of these framed and hung them on the walls of my bedroom where they remained until they eventually disintegrated – they were done on pages torn from my drawing book and it is surprising how long they survived.

Stephen Crane was, also, a friend of my Father but he died when I was too young to have any clear recollection of him. Nevertheless, it was he who gave me my first dog. I have been told that, upon hearing of my arrival into the world he said: 'Good Heavens, the boy must have a dog!' And a dog the boy duly had. He was a sturdy, short-legged animal, square-built, with a shaggy white coat and equipped with a fantastically bushy tail, a black mask, and a large black spot in the middle of his back. One would have thought an animal answering to this description must, inevitably have been christened Spot but in fact, he became Escamillo. This came about as a result of my Father's habit of whistling as he paraded up and down the garden path for what he called his quarter-deck walk. His repertoire was limited to the music of the two operas, *Carmen* and *Cavalleria Rusticana*; the Toreador song from the former being his favourite, and he often told me the story of the bull-fight. Hence the dog became Escamillo, a name promptly elaborated by me into Escamillo Bull-man when discussing his virtues with others, and equally promptly abbreviated to Millo when I wished to attract the animal's attention. As is usually the case with dogs of obscure parentage, he was highly intelligent and became my devoted guardian up to the time when I went away to school. This event coincided, more or less, with my brother's advent into the world so that Millo was able to devote himself to his 'second master' during my absences.

My Father's attitude towards domestic animals was that he approved of them in general and had a moderate affection for our own. He treated Escamillo with kindness and consideration but it was made quite clear that he expected equal consideration in return. For instance, he would administer an occasional pat on the head or brief scratch behind the ears; but any immoderate display of affection by the dog was strictly out of order. He was also irrevocably excluded from the room in which my Father worked, and from the living-room at meal times. Moreover, he was expected to remove himself promptly from my Father's vicinity when instructed to do so. When we went on our weekly journey to Hythe or drove out to visit friends, Millo was permitted to accompany the expedition if he wished – ON FOOT. The square sturdy animal would gallop along for mile after mile, keeping station exactly under the rear axle of the vehicle, with seemingly inexhaustible energy. His presence was, however, never forgotten by my Father who would pull up when he con-

34

sidered the dog had run far enough, and descend in order to lift him up to the rear seat by my side, with the invariable injunction: 'Hang onto his collar, Boy.' Any inclination on the part of Millo, to refuse the offer of a lift was always overruled by my Father, who had very definite views upon the amount of wear and tear permissible to the animal's pads. However, there is no doubt that complete mutual understanding and appreciation existed between them.

It is perhaps appropriate to mention that, when my Father addressed me as 'Boy' he did not use the word in its general sense, but spoke it as written – Boy – with a capital B, and when he wished to attract my attention from a distance, he would cup his hands round his mouth and hail me – 'Boy-oh-Boy'.

My Mother, however, always called me by my name, but invariably used the word 'Boy' when addressing my Father. For instance, when speaking directly to him she called him 'dear Boy' and when wishing to attract his attention would call: 'Boy dear'.

I have no recollection of ever hearing her address him by name – certainly she never called him Joseph – and, in conversation with friends she always referred to him as Conrad.

R. B. Cunninghame-Grahame was also a frequent visitor, but all I remember about him at this period is his distinguished appearance and the grave courtesy with which he invariably addressed me.

The visitors to the Pent who really made an impact upon me were the Dawson brothers, Ernest and A.J. They arrived in, or rather on, a machine called a tri-car. This early version of the three-wheeler of today was, in fact, our first direct contact with motor vehicles and my Father became as absorbed in its mysteries as I was. It had two wheels at the front,

35

between which was a sort of wicker arm-chair providing quite inadequate accommodation for the large and solemn Ernest. The rear end had only one wheel and resembled a motor-cycle. It was steered in the same way as a tradesman's box-tricycle which meant, in effect, that the driver, from his position at the rear, had to point the helpless passenger in the desired direction. On this occasion it appeared that A.J., having his view partially obscured by the bulk of his brother, had driven the machine off the road and through a hedge, causing, as he told us, certain superficial damage to the hapless Ernest but, fortunately, none whatever to his precious machine. As I remember, my Mother refused to subscribe to this callous view and firmly escorted Ernest into the kitchen to have his cuts and bruises tended, while my Father and I listened quite absorbed, to A.J's recital of the machine's numerous virtues.

This visit certainly inaugurated what one might call the motor-car era in the Conrad family, and it was not long before my Father made it convenient to undertake an expedition to Folkestone, in order to consult with an old crony of his, a white-bearded patriarch named Maltby who had also spent some years of his life at sea. At this time he was occupied with running a garage, which I believe, was the foundation of the present well-known firm of that name. As a result of this visit we were able to hire a 4½ h.p. De Dion. I still remember the driver's name, Haines and his red hair, as clearly as I do the many adventurous trips we made in this vehicle. It provided accommodation for four persons in two seats arranged face to face; the space between being largely taken up by a column bristling with knobs and levers, and surmounted by a kind of sewing-machine handle, which, when wound in one way or the other, induced the vehicle to go in approximately the desired direction. Among other peculiarities, it possessed no reverse gear, an omission which caused some inconvenience when, as was sometimes the case, we took a wrong turning and found ourselves confronted by an inhospitably closed farm gate. Upon these occasions my Father and Haines had to dismount and manoeuvre the machine manually. It also stubbornly refused to climb, unaided, any gradient steeper than that of the average railway bridge with the result that they were compelled to jump overboard and run alongside, pushing vigorously. The joy I experienced from their last-minute leap back to their seats as the machine gathered speed at the top of the hill will be readily appreciated.

I should perhaps mention that the costume chosen by my Father for his motoring expeditions was identical with that used when driving our dog-cart, i.e. grey bowler hat, monocle and havelock. The fact that this was a most unsuitable attire when leaping in and out of a moving vehicle seemed to have escaped him.

During the period in which our survival rested in the hands of the red-headed Mr. Haines we charged through a barbed-wire fence, ran up a steep bank and capsized the vehicle on to its side, and finally rammed the large single acetelyne head-lamp through the wheel of a two-wheeled trap, to the great indignation of the farmer who was driving it. All this without any injury to ourselves or any diminution of our enthusiasm for motoring. The encounter with the farmer's trap did, however, produce an unexpected and, to me, highly entertaining sequel.

The efforts to remove the head-lamp from the car or to extricate it from the wheel of the trap, proved unavailing and moreover, were considerably hindered by the behaviour of the farmer who remained obstinately in his seat, dragging at the reins, and making what he imagined to be soothing noises at the unhappy horse interspersed with some lurid remarks about motor-cars, their inventors and the anti-social scoundrels who dared to encumber His Majesty's highways with such infernal machines.

Meanwhile my Mother and I remained seated in the car: I was completely entranced by the proceedings but my Mother, with her usual unruffled calm, quietly assessed the situation and then mildly put forward the suggestion that the horse be removed from the trap. This eminently sensible proposal registered at once with my Father and Mr. Haines. Unfortunately it also got through to the farmer who broke off his uncomplimentary discourse on the subject of motor-cars and those who used them, and descended from the trap to assist in the operation. He was a bulky man and his absence from the seat rendered the trap 'tail-heavy' so that, as my Father released the horse's belly-strap, the conveyance fell backwards shooting the shafts up into the air. Mr. Haines, who was holding on to one of them at the time, also made an involuntary journey skywards and, to my delight, remained suspended in mid-air for some moments before falling to the ground. There was, however, one beneficial result from all this: the abrupt backward movement of the trap twisted the lamp off the car and thus released it. It was, as usual, my Mother who finally poured oil on the troubled waters, not only by soothing, in some mysterious manner, the outraged feelings of the farmer, but also by comforting the horse with lumps of sugar from her pocket where she always kept a supply for the delectation of our own mare.

Looking back on this adventure I feel sure that her concern for the horse was the final touch which enabled us to

38

part amicably from the farmer. The only material damage resulting from the affair consisted of a few scratches on the wheel of the trap and the destruction of one acetelyne headlamp. The ultimate sufferer being Mr. Maltby, inasmuch as he had to buy a new lamp.

It was not long after this encounter that Mr. Haines, and the De Dion, vanished from the scene. The reason for this is unknown to me, but I feel sure it was not the result of any blame being attached to him for the accident. Had this been the case, I would certainly have heard the matter being discussed and, equally certainly, have spoken up stoutly in his defence. Anyone capable of coping with that column, bristling with knobs and levers, would have been worthy of my unstinted support. Fortunately, there was to be only a temporary interruption in our early motoring adventures which, as was soon to become apparent, had by no means reached their climax. Meanwhile I was much pre-occupied as a result of the abrupt removal of one of my boon companions.

Hunt, the gardener, was, in my Father's words, 'an eccentric old scoundrel' but he seemed very fond of me and therefore, my parents had raised no objection to my being in his company. He would seat himself upon the low wall at the end of the garden and call: 'Come 'ere Tommy' – why Tommy I never discovered – and then lift me onto his knee and tell me the most blood-curdling stories about the Indian Mutiny, in which he claimed to have taken part. While some of the stories may have been true, I suspect most of them were invented with the deliberate intention of frightening me. In this he failed utterly; I think I must have been rather a bloodthirsty child. It is possible his unsuccessful attempts to scare me, induced him to indulge in the peculiar behaviour which resulted in his dismissal. He developed a habit of prowling

39

around, muttering to himself and fondling a murderous looking sheath knife and would pause, from time to time, in his perambulations, to sharpen the weapon upon one of the stone pillars of the granary. I was not impressed by this performance, but was sufficiently intrigued to follow him around and keep him under observation. One day it happened my Mother looked out of the window and saw what was going on. She reported the matter to my Father who rushed out and ordered the old man off the premises at once. He seemed far less distressed at his dismissal than I was, and my Father, who was as unimpressed by my lamentations as he was by Hunt's sheath knife, gruffly commanded me to 'stop that damned bellowing' as he returned into the house. He strongly disapproved of any display of emotion on my part.

A few days later I was proceeding upon my lawful – or maybe unlawful – expeditions through the Orchard, when I came upon Hunt, lurking among the currant bushes. He beckoned me, and when I went to him, took me by the hand and led me through a gate into the lane. I noticed he was grasping his knife and for the first time, began to feel uneasy as he seated himself on the bank and drew me to his side. At this moment my Father, who had come out in search of me, appeared round a corner of the lane. Upon seeing my companion he indulged in one of his very rare outbursts of fury and, rushing forward, seized Hunt who was still clutching the knife, and hustled him some distance along the road, giving him a final shove which brought him to his knees. He then came back and taking my hand, led me home in silence. He indulged in no reproaches, and did not even spare a backward glance at Hunt. Moreover, I am convinced he said nothing to my Mother about this encounter.

Hunt was seen no more in the neighbourhood and as I had many interests about the place, I soon ceased to notice his absence. My Mother was convinced he had been toying with the idea of cutting my throat, and I suppose it is possible he had some such project in mind; the important thing to me is that he did not carry it out.

It was at this time that my Father became concerned about my education, and made arrangements with the vicar, in the more distant of the two villages between which the Pent is situated, to receive me into his small private school at the Vicarage. This, however, necessitated providing a ferry service with the dog-cart, in order to carry me to and fro, but he soon found it occupied too much of his time so the experiment was abandoned. I was very sorry about this; I enjoyed being at school, mainly, I imagine, because it brought me in contact with other children.

The next educational experiment was far less to my liking. I was playing around the farm as usual, when a bicycle swept into the yard bearing a tall cadaverous person with lank black hair, a quantity of which appeared to have migrated to his upper lip, from which it drooped like a forgotten garment on a clothes-line. I took an instant dislike to this individual and, when he enquired of me as to where he could find Mr. Conrad, I had a premonition of impending disaster which proved to be well founded. I fear this unfortunate Irishman, whose name was O'Connor, must have felt very uneasy during the time he was my tutor. I am sure I did my best to obey my Mother's injunction to 'be good' but I was unable to overcome my dislike and, for a time, the future looked very bleak. However it was not long before I discovered that my Father disliked Mr. O'Connor as much as I did. This knowledge served to sustain me and eventually the

41

melancholy fellow departed and was replaced by one of my four maternal aunts, of whom I was very fond. Fortunately she was also my Father's favourite sister-in-law so that the clouds now disappeared from my educational horizon.

Another very close friend, from my Father's bachelor days was Mr. Fountain Hope, who lived at Stanford-le-Hope in Essex where my parents became his near neighbours in the first real home they had after their marriage, but I have no recollection of the Hope family until we moved to the Pent, where Mr. Hope was a frequent visitor. I remember him as a man with an inventive turn of mind, although I cannot recall whether he ever came out with any really startling ideas. In fact there are only two incidents which remain in my memory. The first is a very clear picture of Mr. Hope and my Father spending an entire evening painting the red bricks of the great open fire-place in the living-room, with a colourless fluid, a bottle of which Mr. Hope had produced from his pocket and expounded upon with great enthusiasm. I believe he called it water-glass and, as far as I can remember, it produced the same result as shellac.

The second clear memory is Mr. Hope's even greater enthusiasm over a beverage he invented, as a substitute for his favourite whisky and soda which he had temporarily abandoned. It consisted of half a tumbler of soda-water with about a teaspoonful of Worcester Sauce. His attempts to imbue my Father with an enthusiasm for this beverage equal to his own, met with no success, but in later years, I tried the concoction myself, and found it not only palatable, but very refreshing.

Mr. Hope's son, named Conrad after my Father, was also a frequent visitor. Although several years older than myself, he became my friend and always treated me with the greatest kindness, notwithstanding the significant difference in our ages. I think he was the only person who invariably addressed my Father as 'Captain Conrad'.

It was during one of Mr. Hope's visits to the Pent that our first major motoring adventure was conceived. He and my Father were seated on either side of the big open fire-place, deep in consultation while I was squatting, as usual, on the hearth-rug between them, possibly intent upon some mechanical toy, or re-reading Lear's *Rhymes of Nonsense* or *Alice in Wonderland*. This was my usual custom as it rarely occurred to anyone to send me to bed at a reasonable hour. The conversation of my elders flowing to and fro over my head, received little attention from me, and merely conveyed the impression that we were about to go and spend a few days with the Hopes at their home in Essex, a project by which I was not greatly thrilled. Suddenly, however, it dawned on me that the expedition was to be by motor car. I immediately lost all interest in my own activities and gave the whole of my attention to the conversation. It quickly became apparent that my Father had succeeded in hiring another car and driver to replace the departed Mr. Haines, and that the discussion in progress was, in fact, the detailed planning of an adventure. The itinery, and the times of departure of the Gravesend to Tilbury ferry were carefully considered and it appeared that my friend Conrad Hope was to come and spend a night with us and then join the expedition; possibly so that he could act as pilot through the unfamiliar territory on the other side of the river. When I realized the journey was scheduled to start within the next few days my excitement was intense, and I am sure I must have had some difficulty in getting to sleep that night.

The car, on this occasion was a 12 h.p. Darracq and driven

by the owner, a Mr. Hayward. The vehicle was more modern than its predecessor in that it possessed a steering-wheel, but the column bristling with knobs and levers was still in evidence, though in a modified form. Our association with its owner-driver was to last many years, and it was he, and later on his son, who gave my parents their initial driving instruction and sold us our first, and several subsequent cars. I have a photograph of the launching of this expedition and it appears that I made the journey seated upon the knees of my friend, Conrad Hope, but I have no recollection of this arrangement. I have often wondered how in view of the limited accommodation, my Mother managed to reduce our luggage to a sufficiently small bulk.

We set out upon a Saturday, and all went well until we reached Chatham. Traffic congestion, as we experience it today, did not of course exist, but the streets were crowded with pedestrians. Many of these were seamen from the 'men of war' in the river and it seemed they had made full use of the public houses in the town. Some of them were staggering around happily, quite oblivious of any possible hazards, such as a motor car, and one stepped directly in front of us. Mr. Hayward was unable to manipulate his levers smartly enough to avoid knocking the man down and running over his leg. Immediately all became confusion and the victim's mess-mates, no doubt excited by their potations, crowded round shouting abuse. Fists were shaken and an attempt was made to drag Mr. Hayward from his seat.

Then, as always in cases of dire emergency, my Father took command. He descended from the car; brisk orders were given which were smartly obeyed by the seamen in the crowd, and in a few moments calm was restored, the crowd was pushed back and the victim carefully lifted and laid on the pavement. Fortunately his injuries proved to be trivial.

By the time the law arrived on the scene all was quiet and, after seeing the injured man into an ambulance and giving particulars to the police, we were under way again in a very short while.

It was upon occasions like this that my Father showed himself in his true character. Many people, all far better qualified than I, have written about him from the standpoint of his literary fame, or as he appeared to those with whom he came in occasional contact. My aim is to try to give a picture of the man as he revealed himself to me.

I cannot recall any other event worth noting during the expedition, and the several subsequent journeys undertaken in this car, were equally devoid of incident, although they did increase, if this is possible, our enthusiasm, for motor cars.

Chapter Three

IT WAS ABOUT this time that my Mother became so crippled and was in such continual pain that a major operation on her knee became necessary. Orthopaedic surgery, in those days, was very different from what it is now, and I believe it is true that the surgeon concerned made a mess of the job. The operation was performed in a London Nursing Home in a gloomy street the name of which I do not remember. During its course my Father and I paced up and down the pavement outside the establishment, in complete silence; he clutched my hand firmly, a gesture very rare with him, but gave no other visible sign of anxiety. Had my Mother merely been having a tooth stopped, he would have been in a state of agitation and would probably have smoked a whole packet of cigarettes, but on this occasion he did not smoke.

As soon as my Mother was sufficiently recovered, he decided upon a visit to Capri. I have since wondered why he chose such a distant place for her convalescence, but the fact that Uncle Jack and Mrs. Galsworthy were staying in Amalfi may have influenced him to some extent.

I remember no details of the journey except the actual disembarkation at the island. This involved my Mother being carried down the ship's side into a small boat by two chattering Italian seamen. She was seated on an ordinary occasional chair and had to hold her leg out horizontally with the aid of my Father's silk scarf which he had knotted round her ankle. Even this ordeal failed to ruffle her unshakable composure, but I was terrified. My Father, however, showed no sign of anxiety: I believe he was convinced that seamen, whatever their nationality, were utterly reliable.

Capri at that time, was not the holiday resort it is today and our accommodation proved to be in the home of a peasant family. It was a communal establishment, and we took all our meals with them. The progeny were numerous, in fact I have the impression there were at least eight; the eldest being a priest with whom I became very friendly. The daughter whose duty it was to attend on us, occasionally allowed me to penetrate into the kitchen while she prepared the meals on a charcoal fire. I soon picked up a little of the language from Maria and, on the rather frequent occasions when I asked her what we were having for luncheon, I remember she always made the same reply: '*Zoupa de aqua calda e niente*'. The only doctor on the island at that time had been sent full information about my Mother's operation and visited her daily. It was not long before Dr. Cherrio was on friendly terms with us and he sometimes paid us an unofficial visit in the evening, in order to play chess with my Father.

I sometimes watched them as they sat absorbed in their game. My Father's well-trimmed black beard was in startling contrast to that of Dr. Cherrio. Although equally well kept, his was brown upon one side of his face and almost white on the other. This peculiarity also extended to his hair and the division between the colours was sharply defined. I was told it was the result of having been struck by lightning some years earlier.

As my Mother's condition improved one or two expeditions were arranged, the first being a visit to the Blue Grotto.

48

On this occasion she felt able to join us and, with some difficulty, was helped into the boat. When we reached the Grotto however, the sea became rather rough and my Father decided to turn back in case of possible injury to my Mother's leg.

The first stage of our return journey was made in an elderly tramp steamer, from Naples to Marseilles. As was to be expected, my Father immediately was upon excellent terms with the Captain, so much so in fact, that he and I spent most of our time on the bridge. I greatly enjoyed this brief voyage; my enthusiasm over ships and seamen delighted him just as much as his interest in my obsession about machinery delighted me, and thus the very close bond already existing between us became even stronger. Our visit to Capri took place in 1905, and our return home was expediated by a letter he received from his agent, J. B. Pinker, saying that his presence was needed in order to carry out the final revision of his one act play, *To-morrow*, which was soon to be performed under the title of *One Day More*. Personally, I believe he would have liked to prolong our stay in Capri because he was making good progress with *The Secret Agent* and did not wish to interrupt his work when it was going well. This is one occasion when I can state from my own personal knowledge, the work with which he was currently occupied because I overheard him discussing it with Norman Douglas who was in Capri at that time.

After our return from Capri about the middle of 1905 – the year in which my Father was granted a Civil List pension on the recommendation of Edmund Gosse and William Rothenstein – it soon became apparent that my Mother's operation, the first of many which she was destined to undergo during her life, had been even less successful than Dr.

Cherrio suspected. She was in constant pain, moving about with great difficulty, even with the help of her crutches, and it was some time before the surgeon's assurances that her condition would gradually improve showed any indication of fulfilment. Meantime my Father had been suffering more frequent attacks of gout brought on by his anxiety about my Mother, and our doctor advised him to take another Continental holiday as soon as she felt able to undertake the journey.

On this occasion our destination was Montpellier where we stayed at an Hotel in the central square. A cousin of my Mother's accompanied us to act as companion to her and, included in our luggage was the manuscript of *The Secret Agent* – about which my Father wrote in the copy of the book which he gave to his friend Richard Curle: 'This novel, suggested by the well-known attempt to blow up Greenwich Observatory, is based on two pieces of information; one that the perpetrator was a half-witted youth, the other that his sister committed suicide some time afterwards... As literary aim, the book is an attempt to treat consistently, a melodramatic subject ironically.' The pursuit of this task did not, however, prevent him from devoting a good deal of time to me and in fact, as soon as we settled into our rooms, he and I set out to explore the town. This we did by travelling on the single-deck trams, which were driven at a reckless speed by the most friendly fellows, with many of whom we were soon on the best of terms. We must have covered every mile of the Montpellier tramway system several times; always standing on the drivers' platform, as was then permitted in France.

Some of the drivers would lift me up, seat me on the front rail of the vehicle, and allow me to assist with the controls, while my Father wedged himself firmly against the bulk-head behind us and smoked, occasionally exchanging a few words with the driver or any passenger sharing the front platform with us. My precarious position perched on the front rail compelling me often to clutch the driver's sleeve for support when we lurched round a corner more violently than usual, did not appear to cause him any concern.

These excursions invariably terminated at one of the pavement tables of the café beneath our hotel where I consumed cups of hot chocolate while he sipped a glass of Vermouth.

It was not very long before he added to my daily activities by arranging for me to receive fencing lessons at an establishment on the other side of the Square from our hotel, and this was soon followed by riding lessons at the Military riding school nearby. During these instructional sessions he would sit in one of the seats provided, with his chin resting upon hands clasped over the handle of the walking stick held between his knees, and watch the proceedings. I still possess the programme of a fencing competition in which I took part and also a photograph of myself, dressed with strict accuracy, in the uniform of an Able seaman in the Royal Navy, seated precariously and incongruously upon the broad back of an evil-natured grey mare called Tacine, whose chief ambition, as it seemed to me, was to unhorse me and trample me under her feet.

Sometimes my Mother felt able to attend at my riding or fencing lessons but, for the most part, she remained at the Hotel with her cousin. There was a balcony to her room and they often sat out there, being joined occasionally by an elderly but very charming lady, Mlle See, who had been engaged to teach me French and to give me some general education also in that language, thereby ensuring that my

51

schooling did not suffer too much interruption. I came to be very fond of Mlle See and enjoyed my lessons as much as the riding and fencing.

Although the Hotel was reputed to be the best in the town it was by no means a first-class establishment, even by the standards of those days, and the amenities were somewhat limited. For instance there was only one toilet on each floor, situated at the end of the long corridor off which the rooms opened. It was my habit to play in the corridor while waiting till my Father was ready to take me out, and as a result I was privileged to witness an incident which impressed me greatly at the time.

Owing to the limited toilet facilities it was not unusual for a queue of some four or five persons to form outside the door. On one such occasion my Mother emerged from her room and made her laborious way along the corridor on her crutches to join the others who were headed by a small and dapper Frenchman, equipped with the most luxuriant moustache I ever remember having seen. As soon as he became aware of her waiting there propped up on her crutches, he stepped back smartly from his advantageous position and, with a most elaborate bow, gestured her forward to take his place. He then crowned this act of courtesy by handing her his toilet paper – a commodity not provided by the hotel – before retiring to the rear of the queue.

During our stay in Montpellier a performance of the opera *Carmen* was given by a touring company and, as soon as my Father heard of this, he became very excited and insisted that we should all go to the Theatre. My parents and Mlle See, who was invited to join the party, thoroughly enjoyed the performance and I professed myself equally pleased; but my Father's predilection for the Toreador song and his oft-repeated description of the bull-fight, had led me to expect something far more exciting, and I was, in fact, bitterly disappointed.

At the beginning of this century I believe it was a common practise for parents to dress their male offspring in what are known as sailor-suits, and I was invariably attired in this manner until the time came for me to go away to school. In my case, however, my Father insisted that my uniform should be specially tailored and an exact replica of that worn by able seamen in the Royal Navy. Even the short canvas leggings, as worn by the seamen when on shore duty, were specially made for me, and the cap-ribbon H.M.S. *Victory* together with the gilt anchor badge of an able seaman, were specially obtained. He had the greatest admiration for the Royal Navy and regarded the 'sailor suits' as a vulgar caricature of the genuine uniform.

His high regard for sailors and the ships in which they sailed is apparent in his books and he invariably judged the dexterity or capability of those with whom he came in contact by the high standards to which he had learned to conform during his years at sea. My brother and I were, on occasion, chided for acting in a 'lubberly manner' and exhorted to be 'smart and seamanlike'. I remember very well an occasion when I was driving him and Hugh Walpole in our car: Hugh must have made some critical comment on the speed at which we were going. My Father turned upon him irritably and I distinctly heard his reply: 'Nonsense, my dear fellow, the boy handles this car like a torpedo-boat'. This, from him, was the highest possible praise.

The next picture from those now distant days, is of the period immediately preceding my brother's arrival into the world. This major event took place in Uncle Jack's London flat, which he had put at the disposal of my parents for the occasion, and our arrival at 14, Addison Road was marked by an incident which remains very clearly in my memory.

The flat was equipped with electric light, a method of illumination of which my parents, having always lived in the depths of the country, had had little experience. It must have been late when we took possession, or perhaps the day was dull and foggy; anyway the lights were switched on immediately and provided illumination of unaccustomed brilliance for a period of about ten minutes: then they went out abruptly and left us groping around in darkness. My Father, having indulged in his usual mild expletive of 'damn and blast' and used up the few remaining matches in his possession, announced his intention to sally forth and buy candles – and matches. My Mother, in her calm and unruffled manner, said she had not noticed any shops in the immediate vicinity and suggested that the telephone she had seen as we entered the hall should be made use of in order to solve our dilemma.

The telephone was even more unfamiliar to my parents than the electric light and they both regarded this method of communication with the utmost suspicion. My Mother, was, in fact, frightened of the instrument whereas my Father, although in no way intimidated by it, considered it necessary to hold it at arm's length and bellow at it. On this occasion much explanatory shouting at the mouthpiece eventually produced an official from the electricity company. This individual quickly realized the cause of our predicament and asked my Father for a shilling. His indignation at the man's apparent impertinence in asking for a gratuity and moreover, without having done anything to merit it, was quite alarming and it was some time after the man had inserted the coin in the meter and thus restored our light, before he calmed down sufficiently to have the mysteries of shilling slot-meters explained to him.

During the days of waiting for my brother's birth he devoted himself almost entirely to my entertainment, and upon the first morning after our arrival we set out early in search of adventure, leaving my Mother in the care of her maid who had accompanied us to London. I was immediately attracted by the motor buses which, it seemed to me, gave promise of considerable entertainment. We accordingly boarded one of these vehicles which proved to be plying on the route from Marble Arch to Shepherd's Bush. Seeing that the driver was seated very high up I elected to travel on the upper deck, assuming, rightly as it proved, that I would be able to observe his actions more closely from this vantage point. We took tickets to the terminus and, on arrival at Shepherd's Bush, remained firmly in our seats and purchased tickets for the full return journey. On arrival at Marble Arch we again remained in our seats and booked our passage back to Addison Road.

I was delighted with the expedition and my Father appeared to have found it equally enjoyable; so we repeated the journey on each of the next three days, by which time we were upon excellent terms with the driver, and he occupied the interval at the terminus in explaining the mysteries of the engine to us. This particular bus was powered by a steam engine, a fact of which I was not aware until then, but it turned out that it had been brought to the notice of my Father upon our first journey in a manner which must have caused him considerable discomfort. Being a steam engine, it had a funnel which terminated about the same level as the heads of the adult passengers on the upper deck, and

the evil-smelling fumes issuing from it must have completely
enveloped him at times. My attention being concentrated on
the driver's actions and my head being at a considerably
lower level, I was quite unaware of the suffering he had en-
dured on my account with such stoicism. It was now agreed
we should patronize some of the other bus routes and go
farther afield. This we did and my brother was so considerate
as to delay his arrival long enough for me to acquire a size-
able collection of bus tickets.

Eventually the day dawned when we duly inspected the
new arrival; my Father's only comment as I remember was:
'He seems to be a very long baby'.

The birthday was August 2nd, 1906 and in October of the
same year *The Mirror of the Sea* was published. My Father
had a very special affection for this book – ten years later, in
a letter to his friend Mr. Eugene Saxton (of Doubleday Page
& Co) he writes about it as follows: '. . . Twenty years of my
life went to the making of that book; and such an inspiration
does not come twice in a man's lifetime. I am not so humble
as not to be aware that I have been permitted there to
capture the very spirit of the deep – and I am thankfully
content. . .'

It was not very long after the birth of my brother that we
set out again for a continental holiday, and this time our ultimate destination was Geneva. My Father had clearly overlooked the difficulties and embarrassments of a long railway
journey with a small boy and a very young baby, and I remember his expression of shocked astonishment the first time
my brother was provided with a meal and had his toilet
needs attended to in the publicity of the railway compartment. This had no visible effect upon my Mother's composure
in spite of the fact that she had great difficulty in moving

around except with the help of her crutches, but she must have found the journey very trying.

Our arrival at the Pension in Geneva was immediately followed by the discovery that my brother and I had whooping-cough, and the agitation among the other guests when this became known must have greatly added to the anxiety of my parents. A telegram was sent to summon my Mother's maid to help her, but by the time she arrived I had also developed pleurisy and I followed this up in a very short time by getting rheumatic fever as well. The maid, although loyal and devoted to us, was limited in intelligence, and therefore a great deal of the nursing, so far as I was concerned, devolved upon my Father.

As I began to recover he took charge of me completely and no invalid could have had a more devoted attendant. He shared my room with me and it seemed that he was always at my bedside. He would read to me for long periods and make birds and other things out of sheets of paper which he folded with great dexterity. In particular I remember his ability to make six different objects in succession by the continual folding of the same sheet of paper. His choice of books always met with my approval: I believe he must have read them all during his own youth and enjoyed re-reading them almost as much as I enjoyed listening. Among them were Charles Kingsley's *Greek Heroes*, Fennimore Cooper's *The Last of the Mohicans, Deerslayer, The Pathfinder*, and Capt. Marryat's *Peter Simple, Midshipman Easy*, etc. Some of these volumes, which he must have unearthed somewhere in Geneva, are still on my bookshelves with his signature inside the covers.

When I grew strong enough to leave my bed I believe he must have searched all through Geneva to find the most unlikely mechanical toys for my entertainment. The one I liked best was a funicular railway driven by a small steam engine. When the weather was warm enough he would carry me out to the terrace and install me in a chair at the top of the steps leading down to the garden. Then he would fix up the rails on the stone banister with the pulleys at the top by my side and the steam engine at the bottom. Having got the engine going, he would operate the railway from the bottom, sending up to me in the carriages his cigarette case, matches, or any other things he happened to have in his pockets. As I grew stronger I was transferred to the bottom of the steps and my chair arranged on a box so that I could operate the engine, while he took charge at the top. As soon as I was well enough he managed to hire a dilapidated old sailing boat in which we made several voyages along the shores of the lake, and it was not long before he allowed me to take the helm while he attended to the sails. It seems that the Swiss doctor who attended us took a very pessimistic view of my condition. I remember him as a rotund and hairy little man with drooping eyelids. He had a gold *pince-nez*, dangling from a broad black ribbon, which he balanced on the extreme end of his nose in order to gaze at me dolefully over the top of them while combing his beard with his fingers as he talked to my Father. It was not until many years later that the opinion he gave of my condition became known to me. It was that he considered it unlikely I would live long enough to attain manhood. This verdict must have been a severe blow to my parents at the time but, no doubt, our own doctor was able to reassure them when we returned to England.

Chapter Four

It was about the beginning of 1907 that we finally gave up the tenancy of the Pent and moved to Someries Farm near Luton in Bedfordshire. We only lived at Someries for about eighteen months, and I believe it was not a particularly happy period for the family as a whole. However, it was from here that I went to my first real school, as a weekly boarder, and it was also at this time that I had a pony of my own. Don Roberto (Mr. Cunninghame-Grahame was a frequent visitor and he coached me with my riding. In addition to being a fine horseman he was a first-class shot with both rifle and pistol and we made a range in the garden where we spent a considerable amount of time at target practise, often being joined by my Father.

Another visitor, one of whom I was not very fond at that time, was Ford Madox Hueffer. He was involved in the publication of the *English Review*, the first issue of which was prepared in our home. Ford, for some reason best known to himself, spent the greater part of the night sitting on the stairs correcting proofs while my Father was similarly occupied in his study. Each would periodically abandon his lair in order to visit the other for purposes of argument or consultation whilst my Mother circulated with tea, in tall glasses, with lemon and quantities of sugar.

It had not occurred to anyone to send me to bed and I was able to enjoy the activities to the full. In particular I greatly appreciated Ford's somewhat contradictory exhortations to my dog, delivered in a tired and drawling tone when the animal became entangled in his feet during one of his sorties in search of my Father: 'Lie down'. 'Go away'. 'Oh damn!'

A year or two later a violent quarrel arose between them which virtually put an end to the friendship. I do, however, remember with gratitude the trouble Ford took to seek me out and visit me when we were both on active service in the First World War. *A Personal Record* appeared in the *English Review* under the title of *Some Reminiscences* about this time – probably in this first issue.

Much of *Chance* was written at Someries Farm and *Razuman* – afterwards called *Under Western Eyes* – was begun.

I believe that our brief tenancy of Someries Farm was connected, to some extent, with my Father's financial difficulties at that time and also with a disagreement he had with his literary agent, Mr. J. B. Pinker, but I have little first-hand knowledge because I was left behind as a full-time boarder at St. Gregory's School.

Our new home was in the little village of Aldington in Kent. It was the upper part of a rambling house, the ground floor of which was occupied by our landlord, a pork butcher, whose shop also formed part of the building. The slaughter house and the shed where the bacon was cured, were situated at the back of the house directly under the bedroom windows. The squealing of the pigs on the weekly 'killing' days together with the smell from the old-fashioned curing shed must have been very trying for my Father. Moreover it was not long before he suffered a long and severe illness which became so serious at one time that my Mother felt justified in recalling me from school. I was greatly shocked at his appearance when I went to his room and his recovery was very slow.

In due course I was despatched back to school and, during my absence my parents once more went house hunting with the result that, when my holidays came round again, I found them installed in a house which holds, for me, some of the happiest memories of my life.

Capel House, Orlestone, near Ashford belonged to Mr. Edmund Oliver who then lived in a small house on another part of his property. It is a very attractive house, partly surrounded by a moat and having a very large orchard at the side, both of which features figure largely in my memories of our life there. My parents were soon upon very friendly terms with Mr. Oliver and I remember with gratitude, the kindness of his son – later Mr. Justice Oliver – who used to take me with him on his fishing expeditions in the Royal Military Canal which runs from Hythe to Rye, only a short distance away.

I remained at St. Gregory's School for some time after my parents moved to Capel House, my Father having decided that this was preferable to uprooting me and placing me in a school closer at hand. The distance was too great for me to be able to return home for the brief half-term breaks, so that my first-hand knowledge of the family's activities and the coming and going of my Father's friends was limited to the school holidays.

What struck me most forcibly upon my return at the end of each term, was the very rapid growth of my brother. It seemed that I parted from a baby and returned to find a small boy. After the next absence the small boy had grown even bigger and it soon became apparent that he was beginning to catch me up. I noticed that he received much the same paternal attention and discipline as had been bestowed upon me, was given his first gun at about the same age as I received mine and underwent the same strict instruction in the handling of fire-arms. I believe that, as children, we were both equally devoted to our Father, and it never occurred to us to disobey him at any time.

It is, however, true to say that my brother's world was wider and less thinly populated than mine had been, and that he had friends of his own age whereas I had virtually none. However, we got along very well together and, as he grew older, we shared a happy companionship with our Father whenever I was home. I believe there must have been times when Mother was tempted to regard us as an 'unholy trio', and I think it is true to say that my small brother was usually the instigator of our escapades.

In addition to the impact of my brother I found also that I was becoming much more aware of my Father's friends, and I now realized that, apart from those who I have mentioned specifically, there were others of whom, until now, I had scarcely been aware.

Sir Sydney and Lady Colvin for instance, whose very close friendship with my parents must have dated from my early childhood and Arthur Marwood, a near neighbour, who was a very dear friend and with whom my Father exchanged regular weekly visits; Marwood was also, I think, mainly responsible for the arrival of a miniature billiard table in our home, upon which he taught me to play.

This table was designed to fit on top of the dining-table and leaned against the wall when not in use.

My Father was also fond of the game but he was handicapped by the fact that his eyesight was very poor. It was for this reason that he always used a monocle, a habit mistakenly regarded by some people as an affectation. He was strongly averse to spectacles but occasionally used *pince-nez* which he had great difficulty in persuading to stay on his nose. He was, of course, compelled to use them when playing billiards, which gave rise to a certain amount of unfilial amusement which my brother and I derived from our parent's efforts to retrieve them if they fell on the table when he made a stroke, before they were run down by one of the balls. I fear that two of his younger friends, Hugh Walpole and Percival Gibbon, were also guilty of a similar disrespect on these occasions although they were able to conceal their feelings.

These two really seemed to share in the affectionate companionship which existed between my Father and myself in which my young brother was by now included.

One particular escapade in which I remember Hugh participating occurred at the end of a bleak winter's day. We had become bored with billiards and the table had been restored to its resting place against the wall. Father, having turned out the paraffin lamp over the dining-table and lit the candles which he preferred when we were not playing, wandered restlessly around the room for a time and then produced a really brilliant idea. He arranged all the candlesticks in line down the centre of the table and sent me in search of a further supply to be added to those already in position. He then told me to fetch my brother's air-gun and we spent a happy hour seeing how many candles we could blow out at one time with the blast from the weapon. So far as I remember, Hugh was the ultimate winner; a fact which may have tempered the comments of my Mother the following morning on the subject of candle grease on the polished table – she was very fond of Hugh. I cannot recollect if my brother was present at this performance, but I suspect he had already gone to bed; otherwise I am sure he would have thought up some quite devilish amendment to the game.

Of all my parents' close friends, Percival Gibbon, known to my brother and me as Uncle Reggie, was the one with whom I became most intimate; although his habit of taking me on the back of his powerful motor-cycle drew forth a certain amount of adverse comment, particularly when he drove us into one of the dykes on Romney Marshes which he had mistaken in the moonlight, for a continuation of the road.

My affection for Uncle Reggie became even stronger as a result of our meetings in France in the First World War – during which he was correspondent for the *Daily Chronicle*.

After the War our friendship continued right up to his death, by which time he had deliberately abandoned, or had been abandoned by, all his other friends and was living in rather squalid loneliness. He was a fine person and, in my view, a great writer of short stories.

In the intervals between the departure and arrival of my Father's friends there were visits of a different kind. The practice of 'calling' on neighbours was taken very seriously in those days, and my Mother, in spite of her physical disability, felt compelled to comply with the prevailing custom. At this time our sole means of transport was a governess cart and pony which she was able to handle fairly well on her own, although she was usually accompanied by the groom. Return visits were the inevitable result of these excursions, to the great annoyance of my Father who usually took shelter in his study. He was, however, hospitable by nature and sometimes put in an appearance. His manners were quite perfect but, when he was on edge after a long spell of writing, the behaviour of some callers was sometimes too much for him. On one occasion, when two particularly dull and boring ladies visited us, he abandoned his work and joined the party. One of these ladies was wearing a pair of long gloves which she eventually removed and, holding them in one hand, she continually drew them through the fingers of the other while making some particularly banal and uninteresting remarks. My Father sat for a time smiling and listening with apparent enjoyment, then leapt to his feet, snatched the gloves from their astonished owner and hurled them into a drawer which he closed with great violence. He then resumed his seat, all smiles and with an expression of polite interest.

Another occasion when he caused some slight consternation was certainly no fault of his. In this case the social exchanges were taking place in the garden when he emerged to take part, arrayed in a pair of white flannel trousers of generous proportions. Having greeted the visitors with his usual elaborate courtesy, he was about to sit down when a wasp penetrated up his trouser-leg and stung him severely. Leaping violently into the air and shouting: 'Damn! Blast! Bring an onion – bring a blue bag!' he disappeared rapidly into the house.

It was about this time that my faithful Escamillo's life came to an end after more than twelve years of unflagging devotion to me and my brother. His strength had been ebbing for some time, but he persisted in trying to follow us around everywhere until he became completely exhausted and had to be ignominiously conveyed home in the wheelbarrow. He was therefore put to rest and, after a decent interval of mourning, we began the search for his successor. In due course we received information that the keeper of the railway level-crossing about a mile distant, had a puppy to dispose of. We immediately went to investigate and arrived

65

to find two reddish-brown animals locked in mortal combat. My brother at once insisted that we must buy the one with the hairless and mangy tail, if only on humanitarian grounds, since it was obvious he would inevitably kill his adversary if allowed to continue the battle. This we did – at a cost of 5 shillings and our purchase was dragged away from his intended victim and carried home. Father, having briefly inspected the animal threw up his hands in despair and retired to his study; Mother, in her usual practical manner, decreed: a bath and a good meal, after which the little beast looked far more prepossessing.

The following day – a Sunday – we were all in consultation choosing a name for the latest addition to the household, but before we had come to any decision we discovered that the 'subject' of the exercise had vanished. Steps were, at once, taken to organize a search party, but before this could get underway, our domestic staff returned from morning service at the village church, the housemaid bearing in her arms a tired puppy who was happily asleep with his head on her shoulder. She explained that he had followed them across the fields to the church, had been captured and tied to the lychgate by means of a piece of cord provided by a member of the congregation, had then, apparently, eaten the cord, penetrated into the church and subsided happily at the Altar rails in order to indulge in an enjoyable scratch! After being ejected by an outraged verger he had vanished, but had been discovered lurking in the churchyard and brought home. Having listened to this account, Father decreed that since the animal had 'made his pilgrimage', he had earned the title of Hadji, which he held with honour and distinction throughout his life.

Eventually he was on far more intimate terms with the

head of the household than his predecessor and even succeeded in penerating within the sacred precincts of the study. The door of this room, although always closed, was seldom latched owing to a defect in the lock. Hadji discovered this and would gently insert his long nose in the crack and ease the door open far enough to inspect the occupant of the room. We were all convinced that the animal was just as aware of the significance of the waggling foot as we were, because sometimes he would withdraw silently; he was able, in some manner, to avoid making any sound with his claws on the polished floor if he considered such a course advisable. On other occasions he would creep into the room and seat himself at the side of the big wing-chair, remaining there, still and patient, until a hand came over the arm of the chair and rested on his head. He would also, at times, join my Father in his 'quarter-deck' walk, pacing solemnly at his heels and turning with him. The mangy and hairless tail had soon developed into a handsome brush which was carried proudly curled over the back.

At this time the visitors to Capel House fell into two categories. Our intimate friends were expected to travel from London to Ashford by the main line service and there change onto the branch line to our local station – Hamstreet – which is situated at the foot of the steep hill leading onto Romney Marshes, where they were met by our 'governess cart'. The more formal visitors were met at Ashford station, usually by Mr. Hayward's car, and driven the five miles to Capel. This involved a certain amount of organization because we had no telephone – in fact there never was a telephone in our house up to the time of my Father's death – so that Mr. Hayward's instructions had to be sent by post or messenger early enough to enable him to carry them out.

I remember one occasion when Mr. Hayward appeared quite unexpectedly at our front door with his car and, on being asked by my Father – who had a gouty foot that day and was not in a particularly sunny mood – what the devil he meant by it? explained that he had been sent by the landlord of the Railway Hotel in Ashford to fetch Mr. Conrad with all speed to speak to the Editor of the *Daily Mail* on the telephone. My Father, having damned the landlord of the Hotel, the *Daily Mail*, and the Editor, in that order, put on his havelock and the inevitable grey bowler and climbed into the car taking me with him. During the journey he speculated aloud upon the possible reason for this summons, breaking off from time to time to damn the Editor some more – I think his name was Bashford. I kept silent, having learned from experience that I was not required to make any comment on these occasions, unless directly appealed to. Upon arrival at the Hotel my Father demanded black coffee and, while awaiting its arrival, indulged in some further speculation. Eventually the telephone call was made and I have a very vivid recollection of his growing expression of indignant astonishment as he listened. Then he broke into speech and declined indignantly and at considerable length to agree to whatever proposal had been put to him. Finally he slammed the receiver back on the hook and, hobbling quickly out of the Hotel, threw himself back in the seat of the car. I was very curious, but my parent's temperature was clearly so near to boiling point that it would have been folly to seek enlightenment at that time. In fact it was not until the next day that I learned the cause of all the excitement had been the arrest of the notorious Dr. Crippen on the high seas. The fact that wireless telegraphy had made this possible was, of course, a 'front page' story and the Editor of the *Daily Mail* had asked my Father to write an article on some aspect of the event. The effect of an incident of this sort upon him when he was suffering from a spell of gout was sometimes quite contrary to our expectations. In this case we naturally expected it to aggravate the attack but his indignation was so great at, as I overheard him telling Mother, the Editor's 'Confounded impertinence in arbitrarily summoning me all the way to Ashford, while suffering from gout, in order to listen to such a bizarre proposal' that it seemed to have the opposite effect and the attack quickly passed off. My Mother had – rather rashly as I thought – ventured to point out that the much maligned Editor could not possibly have known about the attack of gout. This comment was received by my Father in ominous silence lasting probably two or three seconds, then he threw back his head and gave a shout of laughter: his good humour suddenly and completely restored. What the Editor had, in fact, asked him was to write a commentary upon the books which Crippen was alleged to have read during the voyage back to England after his arrest!! – Truly a 'bizarre proposal'.

From 1910 when we moved to Capel House until 1914 it seemed to me that my Father's younger friends were more often around him than those nearer his own age: The Dawson brothers, Jean Aubrey, Perceval Gibbon, Stephen Reynolds and Norman Douglas for example. These were soon to be joined by Hugh Walpole and my Father's very special friend and neighbour – Arthur Marwood.

Finally, early in 1912 came Richard Curle, then about twenty-four years old, who became surely his most intimate friend, and remained so to the end. Among all these Arthur Marwood was, in a sense, the 'odd man out' in that he was a farmer and in no way actively involved with literature.

Nevertheless there was a very strong bond between him and my Father, but the friendship was terminated by his death early in 1916 – a loss which hit my Father very hard at the time.

In his book *The Last Twelve Years of Joseph Conrad* (published by Sampson & Low, 1928) Richard Curle writes: 'They met every week, and I have never listened to more able talk. Marwood was the profoundest critic I ever knew; his thought acted like a grindstone to sharpen the edge of Conrad's genius. The two men had the highest esteem for one another, and to hear them discussing literature was a revelation. Marwood's death in the early period of the War was one of the severest blows Conrad ever received.'

There were, of course, one or two fortunates among our friends, such as the Dawson brothers and Uncle Reggie who possessed their own transport, and would appear unexpectedly from time to time.

Uncle Reggie who lived some thirty-five miles from us, would sometimes arrive at one or two o'clock in the morning and knock on my Father's study window in order to gain admittance, explaining that 'as it was a fine moonlit night' he thought the motor-cycle ride would be enjoyable.

There came a day when he discarded this motor-cycle in favour of a motor car. It was a single-cylinder, eight-horsepower Swift and, although he claimed to be delighted with it, I suspect he found it a very leisurely mode of transport compared with the twin-cylinder Rex motor-cycle which he had used for several years. I think it was Uncle Reggie's acquisition of a motor car which induced my father to 'take the plunge'.

Our first car was a single-cylinder Cadillac two-seater. It is referred to in a letter he wrote to Sir Sydney Colvin concerning a projected visit to him, as follows: '. . . Yes, we have the little car. It is a worthy and painstaking one-cylinder puffer which amuses us very much; but a journey of eighty miles is not to be undertaken lightly on the back of such an antiquity. . .'

However, he soon revised his views and a journey of eighty miles came to be regarded as a mere local trip.

This machine had epicyclic gears and could be operated by a person using only one foot, so that my Mother was able to learn to drive it. By reason of her placid temperament she was a far better driver than my Father. Our groom was also taught to drive and was promoted to the rank of chauffeur. My own initial experiments in driving were handicapped by the fact that I could not reach the controls when seated, and therefore had to stand up propping my posterior against the edge of the seat and clinging to the steering-column. However, I was managing pretty well, but my Father decided the seat was also too high for Mother's comfort, and called in the services of the village carpenter to lower the seat and also to construct a dicky seat which was supported by four spindly iron legs above the tail-end of the car, in which the engine was concealed. This seat was usually occupied by the newly promoted chauffeur, who was a very tall and lanky youth, so that he gave the impression of towering above the other occupants.

My time at St. Gregory's School now came to an end and I returned home bearing with me, as sole proof of any academic achievement, a book entitled *The Little Duke*, beautifully bound in red leather and bearing the school crest upon it. It was also signed inside by the headmaster in an incredibly neat but quite characterless hand.

The fact that I received this prize in recognition of an

71

alleged proficiency in the study of Holy Scripture appeared to cause my Father some amusement. Quite recently it occurred to me to search out this volume in my book shelves. The characterless signature, although somewhat faded, is just as I remember it, but it belies the very vivid picture of the man himself which remains with me, particularly his habit of bursting into the classroom each morning with gown billowing in the draught caused by the violently opened door, moustache bristling, mortar board perched precariously on the back of his head, *pince-nez* swinging wildly on their cord and cane clutched firmly in his right hand. His rapid entry terminated at the ancient harmonium, upon which he immediately struck a cord with his left hand and burst into song using the cane as a conductor's baton. It was invariably the same hymn: 'All things bright and beautiful, all creatures...' 'Sing louder, little boy' this with a back-handed swipe at the unlucky culprit, and so on to the end; it was perhaps fortunate for us that he always restricted the performance to one verse. Even so everyone within range of the cane had received treatment before its conclusion. We were required to stand in line beside the harmonium so that, inevitably, that portion of the parade which was beyond range of the cane was always appropriated by the senior members of the class.

My education was now interrupted for a period, mainly I think, because my Father was undecided as to where to send me. Meantime I was provided with a tutor in the person of a large and shaggy young man – James Douglas – who had been an assistant master at St. Gregory's School when I was there. In addition to endeavouring to instil a little learning, it was also his duty to try and ensure that I did not break my neck on the decrepit second-hand bicycle I had recently acquired, and upon which I careered about the lanes in a most reckless manner.

J.D. was also provided with a bicycle of sorts in order to enable him to keep track of me but he was not an athletic type and was rarely able to catch up with me except when I had fallen off or ridden into a ditch.

Possibly the strain imposed upon him by this part of his duties accounted for his failure to prepare me sufficiently for the entrance examination at Tonbridge School for which I sat – and failed.

I do not think that my Father was very disappointed; in fact I believe he did not really like the idea of sending me to a conventional school. At any rate, within a short time of hearing the result of the examination, he called me into his room one morning and asked me if I would like to go to the Thames Nautical Training College – H.M.S. *Worcester*. This was music to my ears and the fact that he was so obviously delighted at my reception of the proposal, added to my pleasure.

Unhappily the medical examination, which was an essential preliminary to my acceptance as a cadet, disclosed the fact that I was very short-sighted and would have to wear spectacles. This was a severe blow to me and also to my Father. Moreover, it put an end to any ideas of entering the Merchant Service or joining the Royal Navy – the wearing of spectacles was, in those days, an insurmountable bar to either. In fact there was some doubt as to whether I would even be accepted in the 'Worcester' and my Father decided to pay a personal visit to the ship – which was then moored in the Thames off Greenhithe and seek an interview with the Captain-Superintendent, Sir David Wilson-Barker, R.N.R. At this crisis in my affairs Uncle Reggie stepped in, and

73

offered to accompany my Father and support his plea for my acceptance as a cadet. Reggie had, himself, managed to squeeze a few years at sea into his crowded and adventurous life, and was an enthusiastic supporter of the idea that I should be allowed to complete the training period in the *Worcester*. I was overjoyed when they returned to report the complete success of their expedition, which also proved to be the beginning of a very close friendship between my Father and Sir David.

This obstacle in the plans for my future having been overcome, Uncle Reggie suggested that we should have a brief sea-side holiday by joining him and his family in a villa they had rented for a month at Dymchurch – a small village on the Kent coast between Hythe and New Romney. We accordingly piled into – or rather onto – the Cadillac with the necessary equipment for a short stay, and I was permitted to drive it to Dymchurch. This part of the Kent coast was, at that time, practically in its infancy as a holiday resort, the only accommodation available being the Ship Inn and ten or twelve small villas forming three sides of a square around an un-prepossessing patch of marsh grass, the sea wall forming the fourth side. The villa rented by Uncle Reggie was next to a rather larger one which was occupied, at the time, by Admiral Jellico's family, and the Admiral himself returned there at week-ends from his headquarters at Dover. The local inhabitants were not, as yet, aware of the commercial possibilities arising from the presence of holiday visitors, but it happened that their enlightenment came during the time of our stay and caused a mild sensation from which we derived considerable amusement.

There were, of course, no public services in the area, such as water or light and, in fact, Dymchurch itself was particularly unfortunate in that there was only one well in the village upon which everyone had to depend for drinking water. The owner of the land on which the well was situated suddenly realized the value of his monoply of an essential commodity and promptly imposed a charge of one penny per bucket of water drawn by holiday visitors. Naturally this caused an uproar, but there seemed to be no alternative to paying. Admiral Jellico, however, had other ideas and a couple of mornings later, as my Father and I were walking across the square on our way to the sands, the Admiral's Crossley limousine swept into view driven, as usual, by a blue-jacket. On this occasion, there was a petty officer seated beside the driver, and attached to the rear of the car was a two-wheeled watercart of the horse-drawn variety as used on the marsh farms in those days, on top of which were two more blue-jackets seated smartly at attention with arms folded. As this equippage came to a halt in front of the Admiral's residence the petty officer jumped from the car and gave an order to the two seamen, who leaped smartly to the ground and began carrying water into the house in buckets, which were hanging on the back of the water-cart. This performance was repeated every day during the rest of our holiday, and although we derived no benefit from the operation we were greatly amused and delighted at the way in which the Admiral had defeated the owner of the well.

Chapter Five

DURING OUR first three years at Capel House my Father wrote several short stories, including *The Partner, The Inn of the Two Witches* and *Because of the Dollars*, original title, *Laughing Anne*; all three were included in the volume *Within the Tides* published in 1915. *Under Western Eyes* was published in 1911, the year which saw the completion of *Chance* – published in 1914 – about which he wrote in Richard Curle's copy: 'In this book I made an attempt to grapple with characters generally foreign to the body of my work'. *Chance* was a financial success, and my Father was enjoying reasonably good health so that it was a happy period in our family life.

I was awaiting, with impatience, the day when I would join the training ship, but had I known what was in store for me during that first term I might not have been so enthusiastic. My Father took me to Greenhithe in the car, allowing me to drive most of the way, and handed me and my sea-chest over to the Quarter-Master waiting on the jetty to receive the new entrants. He was clearly horrified at being confronted by a bespectacled cadet, but, by the time I had parted from my Father, he had recovered sufficiently to shout: 'You! Four eyes!' For the moment I did not realize he was addressing me, so he shouted again and all the other new entrants joined in as chorus. It seemed to me that everyone in the ship spent a large part of their time yelling 'Four-eyes' and I was the butt of all hands during that first term, with the exception of the Captain, the Chief Officer and the scholastic staff consisting of the Headmaster and six assistants, one of whom was the ship's chaplain. The latter was the only one of the school staff who had actually been to sea; having been a R.N. chaplain for many years 'Jock' Pedley was a wise old bird and it was largely due to him that I suddenly found myself accepted by the whole ship's company at the beginning of my second term. He gave no outward sign that he knew what I was going through, and it was not until the time came for me to step up into his form – known as the Third Nautical – that I became aware that he was unobtrusively shepherding another newly-joined youngster through a difficult period, and realized that he had done the same for me.

Later when I was promoted to the select company of Cadet Captains who had a wardroom of their own, vulgarly known as 'The Cow-Shed', 'Jock' was always a welcome visitor. He would drink the revolting liquid, loosely described as cocoa with which we were provided and accept a share of anything we had bought from the ship's tuck shop or had sent to us from home. He never discussed religion on these occasions, but he seemed to possess an intuitive knowledge of the problems which were currently afflicting any of the cadets in our individual divisions and would quietly suggest ways in which we as their Cadet Captains could help them.

The seamanship instructors were all ex R.N. Petty Officers, tough disciplinarians, but universally popular.

The hard life of the training ship soon disposed of any lingering anxiety on the part of my parents resulting from the Swiss doctor's pessimistic views about me, and my increasing knowledge of nautical matters made the bond of companionship with my Father even stronger. He usually

78

made the long journey to Greenhithe in the car, in order to collect me at the end of each term, and I am sure he did this mainly in order to afford me the pleasure of driving the car home. I was at this time still too young to hold a driving licence, but this fact apparently caused him no concern.

On one occasion he was unable to come and fetch me so I made the journey by train and arrived at our local station to find no one there to meet me. As I stood waiting by my kit-bag I saw our car coming fast down the steep hill at the foot of which the station was situated. It swung into the entrance at such a high speed as to lift the inner wheels clear of the ground: my Father was at the wheel arrayed in his usual motoring costume, and I could distinctly see the glitter of his monocle. My alarm, and disapproval of his reckless driving, gave way to complete bewilderment when he made no attempt to stop, but swept round the station yard at the same breakneck speed, waving to me cheerfully *en passant*, and disappeared in the direction of home. Abandoning my kit-bag, I ran out into the road to find the car backed into the grass bank some way up the hill with my Father standing beside it coolly lighting a cigarette. As I arrived breathless at his side he greeted me casually: 'Hello, Boy. This damned thing took charge of me and I was quite unable to bring it to anchor. You had better have a look at it.' As I prepared to crawl underneath the vehicle, he added: 'Take your jacket off first or it will become smothered in grease.' As soon as I had re-attached the brake cable which had come adrift, we climbed in and, after recovering my kit-bag, set off for home in silence and he never made any subsequent comment upon the event.

His complete calm and apparent air of detachment in face of any sudden and unexpected happening, in contrast to his excessive agitation over trivialities, always fascinated me and both of these characteristics sometimes caused a certain amount of amusement to all of us.

There was an occasion when my parents had gone to the village together in the car, which had been behaving in a very temperamental manner at that time, and when they had completed their business my Father was unable to get it started. He therefore decided to abandon it and engaged the station cab for the return journey. This was a decrepit horse-drawn vehicle called a 'Fly'. They were common in the country in those days and were a kind of 'poor relation' of the carriage known as a Landau.

Meanwhile, my parents' prolonged absence had caused some anxiety among the domestic staff and the young chauffeur was organized into a one-man rescue party and despatched to the village on his bicycle. As he descended the hill past the station he encountered the dilapidated conveyance and seeing my parents seated in it, he gazed in astonishment with the inevitable result that he rode into the side of it and collapsed over the top of the door onto my Father's lap as he sat grimly with folded arms. My Mother said that he made not the slightest movement, but remained rigid with arms still folded and monocle firmly in place as he growled between set teeth, 'Damned fool!' Nor did he make any movement or comment as she explained to the embarrassed chauffeur where the car had been left.

In contrast, there was another occasion when he was driving Mother home from a visit to Mr. Marwood and found himself held up by three slow-moving farm carts. With his usual impatience he crowded past the first two, scraping the side of the car on each of them and causing my Mother to suggest that, as they were within a hundred yards of our drive gate it was hardly worth squeezing past the third. Whereupon he threw his arms up and exclaimed, 'Do you think I can't pass a damned wagon?' and at the same time, drove straight into the back of it. Luckily they sustained no injury but merely became partially buried beneath the hay dislodged from the wagon by the impact.

The farmer who rented the land around Capel House was very kind to my brother and me, and allowed us to roam the fields and copses with gun and dog provided we did not alarm the animals or damage the crops. We were happy to give this undertaking which we took great care to honour. It happened, however, that my brother derived more benefit from the arrangement than I did because he had not yet embarked upon his school life and was therefore always at home. Moreover, when I returned from the *Worcester* for holidays, my main desire was to drive the car – anywhere, at any time, and in any weather conditions. My Father certainly did his best to grant my wishes in this respect and always allowed me to drive him wherever he wished to go. It is true that some of these journeys involved a long and boring wait while he conducted his business, but this did not in any way dampen my enthusiasm for driving. Of his regular journeys, the one I enjoyed most was to the Gibbon home, because I was very fond of Uncle Reggie and liked his two daughters although they were somewhat younger than I was. Moreover this was the longest regular journey which we made. I liked also the weekly visits to Mr. Marwood at Water Farm where I was able to spend my time fishing in the trout stream which flowed past the end of the garden.

I have already said that my Father was a martyr to gout, an affliction which beset him before I was born and remained with him to the end of his life. At this time there seemed to be no really effective medical treatment either by way of cure or relief from pain, and there were times when he suffered greatly.

On one occasion when I was at home, he had a particularly painful bout, and our regular doctor being for some reason or other unavailable, he decided to pay a visit to the local one who had only lately arrived in the village. He told me to get the car out and drive him there. I ventured to point out that, during the short time he had been in the district, this medical gentleman had already acquired a reputation for extreme eccentricity, and was told, somewhat sharply, that: 'It doesn't matter a damn how eccentric he is if he can provide some relief from this infernal pain', so I got the car and we set out for the village.

At this point it is necessary to mention that my Father had difficulty in pronouncing certain words in English, and there were those who wrote about him as having a strong foreign accent, but I consider this to be a gross overstatement. Nevertheless, it is true that, when unwell or under emotional strain his mispronunciation became more marked. We in the family were, of course, familiar with most of the words with which he had difficulty but occasionally one would crop up which was not known to all of us. This happened after our visit to the doctor and, for a short time, caused me acute distress.

In due course my Father emerged from the doctor's house and resumed his seat in the car in silence. We set out on the homeward journey and after a while I ventured to enquire: 'What did the doctor say?' The reply hit me like a physical blow: 'Oh! Of course you are dying.' I felt unable to make any comment and immediately on arrival home, went in search of my Mother. She naturally noticed my agitation and enquired what was the matter. When I told her what my Father had said to me, she smiled in her usual gentle manner and, putting her arm round my shoulders said: 'Don't worry, dear. He didn't say, "You are dying", he said, "iodine", he always pronounces it "uredyne".' At that time the painting of the affected joint with iodine was the most common treatment prescribed, and his inability to pronounce the word was unknown to me until then.

My Father must also have noticed my agitation, and when Mother took his tea in to him said that he feared I must 'be sickening for something'. She assured him that I was perfectly well, but he refused to be convinced, and she was compelled to tell him what had so upset me. I was immediately summoned to his room, informed gruffly that I was a 'damned fool', given an affectionate thump on the back and told to 'clear out now'.

Lady Millais lived barely three miles from Capel House and became one of my Mother's closest friends. She had few intimates near at hand and her physical disability deterred her from making long journeys, so that she enjoyed driving the short distance to Leacon Hall once or twice a week to spend an hour or so with Lady Millais. The latter's son, named John like his grandfather the artist, was an invalid at this time, confined to an invalid carriage with tuberculosis. I believe the malady, in the form in which it had afflicted him, was known as hip disease. He was a young man – then in his late twenties – and had been in the Navy, reaching the rank of Lieutenant. My Father and I became very fond of Sir John Millais (he had inherited the Baronetcy originally conferred on his grandfather) and one or both of us would often go with Mother when she visited her friend, and spend the time sitting by the invalid carriage or, in my case, wheeling it slowly around the garden while its occupant talked with unfailing cheerfulness, of his life in the Navy, or plied me with questions about my own life in the *Worcester*. He had, like the majority of Naval Officers, passed through the training ship *Britannia* which at that time was part of Dartmouth Naval College, and he enjoyed comparing my training-ship experiences with his own.

My Mother and Lady Millais remained close friends throughout their lives but Sir John's life was already approaching its end and I shall therefore tell now of my last meeting with him.

My unit was in Barracks at Portsmouth towards the end of 1915, awaiting orders to go overseas, and I and several other officers had been dining at a popular restaurant in Southsea. As we came out into the street a car pulled up sharply and a young Naval Lieutenant leaped out and grabbed me by the arm. To my utter astonishment it was John Millais, looking very fit and in the best of spirits. He begged me to join him for a while, so I hastily parted from my companions and re-entered the restaurant with him where, over coffee and brandy, he told me he had that day seen the C.-in-C. Portsmouth, had been accepted for active service, and was now awaiting posting to a ship. I asked him about his health and he replied airily 'Oh! I just got well again.' Many times during my life I have speculated upon the amount of courage and grim determination concealed within those few words. To all intents and purposes he must have 'willed' himself out of that invalid carriage and talked his way back into the Navy!

We spent an hour or so together and agreed upon another early meeting but I never saw him again. We received our orders the following day and before I had been in France quite twelve months, I received a letter from my Mother telling me that Sir John was home and on his back again. He died before my final return home. I feel sure the memory of his escape from that invalid carriage and brief return to the Service to which he was devoted must have helped him through the last days of his life.

When my period of training in the *Worcester* came to an end, I was able to return home, bringing with me a First Class Certificate. To qualify for this it was necessary to pass examinations at the same level as is required in order to obtain a 'Master Mariner's Certificate' in the Merchant Service. Moreover the holder was entitled to count his two years *Worcester* training as one year's apprenticeship at sea, thus reducing the usual four-year apprenticeship to three, after which he would be able to take the examination for 'Second Mate's Certificate'.

None of this was any benefit to me as I was unable to go to sea, but it delighted my Father and he cherished that piece of parchment to the end of his life.

It was at this time that we said goodbye to the faithful little 'one cylinder puffer'. I believe we all had a sense of gay adventure whenever we went out in this sturdy little car and, for my part, I had a very strong feeling of personal loss at its departure. It also put an end, at least officially, to my Mother's driving. I say 'officially' because there was one occasion when she and I shared a small private escapade in its successor. This was a ten h.p. Humber four-seater touring car, whose only peculiarity was the fact that its engine was designed to run anti-clockwise, with the result that everyone experienced some difficulty at first, in starting it – there was, of course, no self-starter.

I sensed that Mother was regretting the change of cars, and

one evening, when I was sitting with her in the room we called 'The Den', it occurred to me to ask her if she would like to come for a short run with me and try her hand at driving. She jumped at the idea, so I went to get the car while she wound a scarf round her head. It was quite late by this time and everyone was in bed except my Father who was working in his room at the other end of the house, so we crept out quietly. The Humber had bucket type front seats and the controls were on the right so that it was impossible for Mother to scramble in from that side. Instead she had to get in on the left and move across the car into the driving seat. I stood on the right-hand step in order to manipulate the handbrake and gear lever, hanging on to the back of her seat with one hand. She operated the clutch with her one service-able foot and used the hand accelerator on the steering wheel to start away. The land on which Capel House stands is bounded by three lanes and a section of the main road making a total circuit of about two miles which was used by us as a sort of test route. We accordingly set out on this circuit and, as soon as we had jointly got the car into top gear, I told Mother to transfer her foot to the accelerator pedal. This she promptly did, and pressed – hard – just as we arrived at the first of the four turns in the circuit. We negotiated this turn on two wheels and I came very near to being dislodged from the step and left behind in the ditch. I yelled at her to lift her foot off the pedal but she took no notice and seemed to have got the bit firmly between her teeth. By this time we were right upon the second turn and I managed to reduce the speed sufficiently with the handbrake to enable us to keep all four wheels on the ground. As soon as I released the brake we again leaped forward but I was able to persuade Mother to lift her foot at the third and fourth turns, after which she

86

had a relapse, and slammed her foot down again – on purpose I believe – with the result that we shot past our drive gate and embarked upon a second circuit. Fortunately, the country folk went to bed very early in those days and so were spared the terrifying spectacle of a motor car hurtling along the moonlit lanes driven by a stoutish lady with head scarf streaming behind her in the breeze and having, apparently, a smallish male companion crouching by her shoulder. The second circuit was accomplished at a more reasonable speed but I insisted upon returning while we, and the car, were still intact. After putting the car away I re-entered the house to find Mother placidly preparing the tea which, served with lemon instead of milk, was our invariable nightly drink, I therefore went into the 'den' and soothed my nerves with a much needed cigarette, which reminds me: when I first went to the *Worcester* my parents extracted a promise from me that I would not smoke before I was fifteen. There was a lot of smoking going on in the ship but I kept my promise and, on my fifteenth birthday they presented me with a silver cigarette-case, a silver match-box and one hundred cigarettes. I remember there was considerable envy among my messmates when I exhibited these gifts in the privacy of the 'Cowshed'.

It was now decided that the next stage in my education should be an attempt to secure a place at Sheffield University and make a bid for a B.Sc.(Eng.) degree.

The curriculum in the *Worcester* was restricted to the main objective of producing a good seaman and potential ship's officer, and it was clear that I would need to widen my field of knowledge very considerably. I was therefore despatched to a tutor in Upper Norwood, who took resident pupils. There were about a dozen of us, and the Tutor, whatever his academic qualifications may have been, was no disciplinarian, so that we did pretty much as we liked, made a general nuisance of ourselves in the neighbourhood and, so far as I was concerned, learned exactly nothing. The result was that my attempt to get accepted ended in failure. My Father accompanied me to Sheffield when I went to sit for the examination and, on the last evening before we returned home to await the result, he suggested I might like to go to the Variety Show at the theatre. I accepted gladly and then found, to my astonishment, that he intended to accompany me – it was not the sort of entertainment anyone who knew him, would have expected him to attend, and I had serious misgivings as to the outcome. The first turn proved to be a troupe of acrobats which he applauded vigorously – he always appreciated exhibitions of skill. An inferior comedian followed, and was glared at in grim silence. Next came a male singer surrounded by a bevy of scantily clad females. This collection was gazed at with an expression of incredulous disgust. Then came the principal turn of the evening: George Robey. I felt sure this would prove too much for him, but the first few jokes appeared to produce no reaction. Then George got into his stride – he was in very good form that night – and the house rocked with laughter and applause. Weird noises began to emerge from the still figure at my side and I braced myself for the sudden and violent exit which I felt to be imminent. Nothing happened and eventually the audience allowed George to leave the stage, the lights went up and I realized that my Father had, in fact, been convulsed with laughter!

He was very distressed when the news of my failure to pass the examination arrived, but decided that I should make a further attempt when we returned from a visit to Poland which he had arranged.

Chapter Six

My FATHER had not re-visited the country of his birth since some years before his marriage in 1896, and of course, the family had never been there. A young Polish friend of his – Dr. Joseph Retinger and his wife, Tola, were to travel with us and we were to spend a part of our visit at Tola's family home – Goszcza.

By this time the First World War was close upon us but my Father refused to be put off by what he described as alarmist rumours, and we set out during the last days of July 1914 via Germany. We spent one night in Berlin and, the following day being Sunday, we paid a visit to the Zoological Gardens before taking the evening train to Vienna and then on to Cracow where we were to wait until Tola, who had gone on ahead to prepare for our reception, returned to escort us the last twenty or thirty miles to her parents' country estate. The journey was without incident so far as I can remember, except for the somewhat hostile attitude of an attendant at the Zoological Gardens when he realized we were British.

We arrived in Cracow early in the evening and had time to bath and change our clothes before going into the dining-room for dinner. A table had been allotted to us on the far side of the room, and when we were about half-way through the meal, I suddenly became aware of my Father sitting quite rigid, with his fork half-way to his mouth, staring across the room towards the door. I turned to see what had attracted his attention in this way, and the picture which remains in my memory is of a tall handsome man with grey hair and moustache, standing motionless in the doorway and staring with equal intensity. Before I had a chance to ask the reason for this performance, my Father dropped his fork and leaping to his feet with a shout of 'Kostoosh!' rushed towards the door. His opposite number in the doorway burst into violent motion at the same time, and they met and embraced in the middle of the big room. When their mutual emotion had subsided somewhat, they came to our table and the stranger was introduced to us as an old school friend of my Father's – Mr. Buszinski. He remained with us for the rest of the evening and, before leaving, invited us to spend the following day with him at his country home a few miles from Cracow. With the assistance of the hotel manager, we were able to hire a car for this expedition. It was an old Lorraine-Dietrich touring car with a vast expanse of rear seat equipped with a leather hood similar to that of a perambulator. There was also a canvas attachment which buttoned onto the front of the hood and extended to the top of the windscreen to give quite inadequate protection to the driver.

It was during the course of this visit that the war burst upon us. We had spent an enjoyable day and were preparing to return to the hotel, when a troop of Austrian cavalry rode up to the house and proceeded to commandeer every horse and vehicle on the premises. My Father and his friend had the greatest difficulty in persuading the officer in charge to refrain from commandeering our hired car and I think he only did so out of consideration for my Mother who, fortunately, emerged from the house at just the right moment, supporting herself with her two walking-sticks.

We returned to the city to find it completely transformed by the Austrian mobilization. Horses and vehicles had, for the most part, been absorbed by the army and a rash of uniforms had appeared among the populace. Even our hotel manager, who had seen us off in the morning beautifully arrayed in frock-coat and striped trousers, now came out to greet us in the uniform of a Captain.

We had expected to find Tola awaiting us at the hotel but she had not arrived. Her family home was several miles beyond the frontier between the Austrian and Russian parts of Poland and some anxiety was felt as to her safety. This was greatly increased when Retinger, who had gone out to try and get some news about the general situation, returned with the alarming information that the Russian frontier guards had withdrawn twenty miles into their own territory and that the Austrian guards were preventing anyone from crossing the frontier. After some discussion Retinger decided to go out to the frontier in the hired car which was still outside the hotel and try to bribe the guards to send a messenger to Tola's home and, if possible, get her to return with him to the frontier post. My Father reluctantly agreed to this rather 'forlorn hope' enterprise and said that I should accompany him. Joseph (Retinger) at once went off to organize the expedition and my Father took me aside and explained that he was letting me go because he wished me to try and restrain Joseph from making any foolhardy attempt to get across the frontier himself. When Joseph returned to say that all was ready he had managed to secure two revolvers, one of which he passed to me, but my Father, who had his eye on us, promptly impounded the weapon and also persuaded Joseph to relinquish his, saying, very wisely, that we would be far safer unarmed. He then came out to see us off.

91

When we arrived at the frontier post, Joseph explained the situation to the officer in command and, as my Father had expected, made a strong plea to be allowed to go on himself in search of Tola. He was promptly told that, in no circumstances would he be allowed to go any further and that if he made any attempt to do so he would be shot.

The officer was, however, very friendly and sympathetic and invited us into his own room where we were given some food and coffee – also a bottle of Vodka was produced. This was my first introduction to it; in fact my first experience of 'hard' liquor and resulted in the discovery that I could take a considerable quantity of alcohol without any noticeable effect. We must have consumed most of the bottle during the course of the night and Joseph was plainly affected by it, no doubt, because of his great anxiety about Tola. The officer, who had left the room as soon as the refreshments had been brought in, came back after about an hour and began talking urgently to Joseph. As he spoke in Polish, I was unable to understand a word and had to wait as patiently as possible until Joseph could translate for me. It appeared that he had sent two of his men forward into Russian territory in order to try and contact one of the local inhabitants. In this they were successful and returned with a terrified peasant whom they had, as he thought, taken prisoner. This man was brought in and interviewed by Joseph, who offered him a considerable sum of money if he would take a message to Tola's home. He agreed and set off at once with a note for Tola; Joseph also gave him half of the agreed payment and promised the balance if he returned with her.

We now settled down to wait with as much patience as we could muster and the officer, having now realized that I did not speak Polish, very considerately carried on all further

92

conversation in French for my benefit. The night passed slowly. I played chess with one of the frontier guards and Joseph prowled up and down the room; the officer wrapped himself in his greatcoat and slept on the floor. With the coming of dawn it became obvious that our bid to rescue Tola had failed. The peasant must have either taken the money and returned to his home or been picked up by a Russian Cavalry patrol, two of which we could see in the distance through field-glasses. The officer and I finally prevailed upon Joseph to return to Cracow and the former promised that if any news did come in, he would send a courier to the hotel. My parents and my young brother were very relieved to see us safely back – my Father had been pacing up and down the hotel vestibule all night.

For the next few days we were allowed to move around with only the minimum of restriction, and my Father made the most of this opportunity to contact as many influential Polish people as possible – not that he had any hope that we should be allowed to leave the country, but in order to try and make our enforced stay as comfortable as possible. I accompanied him everywhere and he found time to show me around Cracow, the Cathedral, and the University. Also the house where he had lived for a time as a small boy with my Grandfather. He, of course, spoke Polish all the time and, when he had occasion to speak to me in public, did so in French, which caused no comment – it appeared to me that all Poles spoke French fluently. We had lost most of our heavy luggage somewhere along our route so that there were a number of embarrassing deficiencies in our wardrobes. For instance my Father had, apart from the suit he was wearing, four pairs of white flannel trousers and a tail-coat; also fortunately as it proved, his 'gout-boots'. Mother was the worst off as she was unable to buy anything to fit her. There was, however, no difficulty in providing for my brother and me. Among the luggage remaining to us was my pocket Kodak camera and several rolls of film so I loaded the camera and carried it around in my pocket when accompanying my Father. I took some excellent photographs of the Cathedral and University, also several of scenes during the first few days of the Austrian mobilization; no one seemed to take any notice and the danger of what I was doing did not occur to me nor, surprisingly, did my Father appear to realize the possible consequences.

Mother was stubbornly determined to locate our lost luggage and to this end she coerced the unfortunate hotel manager, who had not yet left to join his unit, into making extensive but fruitless enquiries of the railway authorities. Eventually some other people came to the hotel having just travelled from Vienna. They told us that all the stations in the City, I believe there were three, were piled high with lost luggage and that no steps were being taken to sort it out. My Mother therefore abandoned the search but she was by no means defeated. There was a cousin of my Father's, Mme Zagorska, who had a Pension in the village of Zakopane, up in the Tatra mountains, and eventually the authorities agreed we should be sent there and allowed to live as guests at the Pension.

Soon after our arrival in Zakopane Tola rejoined us having managed to get back across the Austro-Russian frontier and we soon settled down to an enjoyable routine. The place was quite beautiful and, although we were officially confined to the village, we were able to organize some climbing parties under the care of a Dr. Gorski. My brother found friends of his own age among the other guests and Mother enjoyed the companionship of Mme Zagorska and Mme Kosch who occupied the room next to that of my parents. My Father suffered the most at this time; the impossibility of communicating with Mr. Pinker – his literary agent – or with his friends in England, worried him greatly and he found it impossible to settle down to any writing. It became a regular routine for me to accompany him every morning to the principal café where everyone gathered to discuss the War and their own personal problems over coffee or a drink.

There was an acute shortage, locally, of small currency; in fact practically the only coin in circulation was the *pfennig* – at that time about the size of our farthing. They were an embarrassment when carried in quantity in the trouser pocket and it became the custom to roll them up in a sheet of paper, one hundred at a time, and twist up the ends, thus forming something similar to a pen or pencil.

These were carried in the breast pocket of one's jacket. The idea worked well enough up to a point, since each stick represented one 'crown', but when a part of that value was needed it became necessary to break off a portion, which usually resulted, in my Father's case, in an avalanche of small coins falling to the floor of the café, from whence it was my privilege to rescue them.

There now came a period of activity among his Polish friends with whom he was once more in almost daily consultation and eventually he told me he was trying to get a permit for us to travel back to Vienna where he planned to enlist the help of the American Ambassador in the hope that he might at least be able to communicate with his agent, Mr. Pinker. He warned me to say nothing to Mother in case he was unsuccessful – he need not have bothered – I discovered that she was perfectly well aware of his activities.

At last with the help of Mr. Kosch we obtained a permit

from the Military Commandant of Cracow – a few words written on the back of one of his visiting cards which authorized us to return to the city where arrangements would be made for us to travel on to Vienna.

Mother spent the evening packing up our remaining possessions, my Father was engaged in organizing transport for the first part of the journey, and I crept out into the cold darkness of the garden in order to bid an emotional farewell to one of the young female fellow-guests with whom I imagined myself to be desperately in love, and whose name I don't even remember.

We set out at midnight, during a heavy snow-storm, in an open carriage drawn by a pair of wild and shaggy horses, urged on with voice and whip by an equally wild and shaggy peasant, who appeared to think we were being chased down that mountain road by a pack of starving wolves. Fortunately, the darkness and the weather concealed from us most of the hazards which must have been encountered on that journey.

When we arrived in Cracow we went back to the hotel. The friendly manager had, by now, gone off to face whatever the fates had in store for him on the battlefield and his place had been taken by a much older man. There were a number of army officers billeted in the hotel and we found it very different from when we first stayed there.

My Father went at once to see the Military Commandant and was told that the necessary travel permit would be sent to us at the hotel the next day. Several of our Polish friends came to see us during the course of the evening, and we heard from them that there was a lot of cholera among the troops. Upon hearing this my Father decided that we should carry our own water supply on the journey to Vienna and asked one of his friends to secure water bottles for us. In due course he returned with four army-type water bottles – I suspect they were later found to be missing from one of the military stores in the city – which my Father had filled with boiled water under his own supervision. My young brother carried one strapped on his back like a haversack. Meantime Mother arranged with the manager for some food to be packed for us, so that, when the travel-permit was delivered, as promised, in the morning, we were ready to go to the station and await the train – in fact we waited nearly all day – and when it did arrive it proved to be full of sick and wounded troops; among the former we heard there were some cases of cholera. One of the Commandant's Aides was at the station to supervise our departure, and he had one compartment cleared of troops for us. We spent two days and nights in that train before it eventually crawled into Vienna. It stopped innumerable times on the way and on several occasions some of the sick or wounded were removed on stretchers. My Father had obviously acted very wisely in arranging for us to carry our own supplies of food and water. We had practically no sleep during the journey and were thankful to get to a hotel and rest. It must have been a great ordeal for Mother but she remained outwardly calm and placid as always.

The next morning she went into action and announced her determination to search every railway station and goods yard in Vienna for our lost luggage. My Father remonstrated with her in vain – she could be as stubborn as a mule at times – and finally he flung up his arms and stamped out of the room, pausing for a moment before slamming the door to tell me: 'Go with your Mother Boy and take care of her.'

It was clear that this operation was going to prove very

97

difficult – for one thing Mother spoke no foreign language nor could I speak German, and my French, although good, was unlikely to be of much help in questioning the Austrian railway officials. I therefore went and asked the hotel porter if he could find me a cab-driver who was able to speak English or French well enough for our purpose. After some time he reported that he had been successful and that the man was already waiting at the entrance with his cab. We went out and were introduced to an individual who certainly spoke with great fluency – in a mixture of English, and French with a few words of German interspersed. As this seemed to be the best we could expect, we decided to start at once, and I helped Mother into the dilapidated cab and took my place at her side. Our interpreter then woke up the emaciated quadruped between the shafts, which vaguely resembled a horse, climbed up to his seat and we set off upon our search.

I don't remember how many stations and goods depots we visited without even a glimpse of hope, but Mother refused to be discouraged by the vast piles of trunks and suit-cases, many of which had burst from the weight of those piled on top of them and disgorged their contents. Finally, when I had become nearly as exhausted as the unhappy animal which was dragging us around, we arrived at a huge cavern of a railway shed stacked to the roof with luggage of all shapes and sizes. I tried to convince Mother that it was madness to imagine we could search through this fantastic conglomeration, but before I had said a dozen words she gave an exclamation and walked to the other side of the shed. I followed to continue my remonstrations and found her pointing with one of her sticks at a brace of flattened cabin trunks which I recognized as ours.

They were, of course, right at the bottom of the pile and the few railway people present flatly refused to contemplate extracting them for us until Mother opened her bag and produced an English sovereign. British gold still held its magic in those days – even in enemy country – and the remnants of our two trunks were loaded into the cab in a surprisingly short time.

When we got back to the hotel my Father expressed no surprise at our success, and merely remarked that he 'hoped his suits were not completely ruined'.

During the days that followed I accompanied him to the American Embassy and he was able to see the Ambassador – Mr. Penfold who was most helpful and did, I believe, arrange for some news about us to be sent to the U.S. from whence it was eventually passed on to England. What was more important is that through his influence, we eventually secured a permit to leave the country and cross into Italy. However, this took some time and during the period of waiting we were able to see something of Vienna, although we had to be far more circumspect in our movements than we had been in Cracow where we were among Polish people who regarded my Father as a fellow-countryman and took pride in his reputation as an English writer. However, the Austrians treated us very well and put no irksome restrictions upon our movements. We all went for one or two drives about the city and once even caught a glimpse of the old Emperor, Franz Josef, passing in his carriage with a cavalry escort.

My Father and I went about together a lot as usual, and one day as we wandered through the streets, he suggested we should patronize a shooting gallery which seemed to be attracting a lot of customers. When we got inside, however, we were shocked at finding that this was no ordinary shooting gallery; it appeared to be a sort of War propaganda entertainment. Instead of conventional targets there were cinema screens on which were being shown a film of kilted Scottish infantry charging with fixed bayonets, and the marksmen had to fire at the figures as they ran across the screens. When a hit was made the film stopped and the marksman was invited to choose a prize from the trays of junk displayed. My Father paused and uttered a startled exclamation when he saw what we had walked into, and then gripped my arm and urged me forward saying: 'We have to go through with it Boy, to retract now would draw too much attention, but take care you don't hit any of those fellows.' This admonition was accompanied by one of his most virulent glares. When our turn came he purchased the minimum amount of ammunition – five rounds each – and we took the rifles handed to us. I took a deep breath, hoped for a lot of luck, and concentrated on missing those running figures. My relief at seeing them still running after firing my last shot was abruptly dissipated by my Father who handed me his five cartridges growling: 'You had better use these as well.' I realized that this action on his part was no gesture of paternal affection – he just felt he dare not fire them himself – so I took another deep breath, and, I am thankful to say, succeeded in 'missing' five more times. He would have been terribly distressed if I had hit one of those running figures.

As the days passed, it became clear that he was feeling the strain of waiting and hoping for a permit to leave the country, and Mother, although as always she gave no outward sign of anxiety, told me that she feared an attack of gout was imminent. I had also been expecting something of the sort, and we were greatly relieved when at last a message came asking my Father to call at the U.S. Embassy. Although I went with him, I was not actually present during his interview with the Ambassador. All I know is that a document was provided which was to enable us to travel to Udine, on the Italian Frontier.

Before setting out on this stage of the journey which, although long and tedious, was without incident, our water bottles had been refilled and a supply of food packed for us by the hotel. So far as I remember it was early morning when the train eventually reached the frontier and my Father at once alighted and went to present his papers at the Austrian frontier post, taking me with him. We found that the Austrian troops had been withdrawn from duty and replaced by Germans. This, as we heard later, had been done on direct orders from the Kaiser's headquarters with the object of tightening up the restrictions against people trying to leave the country. A Prussian non-commissioned officer took our papers and, after a casual glance handed them back with a contemptuous gesture which clearly indicated that he considered them unacceptable.

My Father had always insisted that he could only speak a few words of German, however, in this emergency, it seemed to me that he spoke at considerable length and with great fluency, but the only effect this had on the Prussian was to cause him to lose his temper and start shouting at us.

My Father eventually shrugged his shoulders and turned away with a gesture of despair, saying 'It's "no go" Boy.' Then he stopped abruptly, put his hand into the breast pocket of his coat and pulled out our British Passport which he opened at the page bearing the German visa that had been necessary to enable us to travel through Germany on the outward journey. He turned back and thrust it under the

Prussian's nose. The result was remarkable – the fellow examined the visa and then clicked his heels smartly and assumed an expression which might conceivably be described as friendly as he handed the passport back to my Father and waved us to our compartment. When discussing his action later we concluded that he must have accepted the visa solely because it was written in German, and overlooked the fact that it was in a British Passport. We were very lucky – far more so than we realized at the time, because after we got back to England, we heard through U.S. diplomatic channels, that soon after we left Vienna, orders came from Berlin to detain Joseph Conrad and his family.

Our train now travelled on to the Italian frontier post and thence into the station at Udine, where we were all confined to the train while the medical authorities satisfied themselves that there was no infectious disease among the passengers. Everyone protested loudly and complained that we were in need of some refreshment after being cooped up for so long. As a result of much shouting and arm-waving this was promised and eventually arrived. It consisted of hot coffee in china receptacles more usually found under the bed, which some Italian girls carried along the platform on their heads. They paused under the carriage windows so that the passengers could – provided they had a cup or glass – scoop up some of the liquid. I noticed that some of them were plunging their cupped hands into the receptacles so we unanimously decided not to avail ourselves of this initial gesture of Italian hospitality.

Eventually the train ambled on to Milan where we decided to stay and rest for a day or so before going on to Genoa from where we hoped to secure a sea passage back to England.

My Father had telegraphed to his agent in London for

money and, as soon as this arrived, we went on to Genoa where he was able to book passages for us in a Dutch Mail boat which was due to call at Genoa in about ten days on her voyage home from the country now known as Indonesia.

Having completed these arrangements he announced that we 'might as well take a look around' and engaged one of the taxis, which waited outside our hotel, on a daily basis to take us for drives up into the hills behind the town. This gave me an opportunity of making use of my last roll of films but I reserved a few exposures for use on the voyage home.

The vessel arrived in due course and we embarked for the last stage of our journey. Before we had been twenty-four hours on board, my Father had, as usual, managed to get upon the best of terms with the Captain and the ship's officers and spent a good deal of his time in the Captain's cabin or on the bridge with the officers of the watch. I was able to get one or two photographs of Gibraltar as we passed through the Straits, and this left me with just one exposure which, very luckily as it proved, I decided to keep in reserve.

Early next morning my Father burst into my cabin and shouted, 'Come up on deck, Boy – hurry!' I snatched up my coat and followed him wondering at his excitement. It was just after sunrise and we were steaming across the Bay of Biscay in a moderately heavy sea. He took me by the arm and, dragging me to the rail, pointed at three British destroyers steaming fast, in line ahead, and rapidly overhauling us, saying: 'Look Boy!' I looked, and then, to his indignant astonishment, jerked out of his grasp and rushed below again – for my camera – I was back within a couple of minutes. His angry glare vanished when he saw the reason for my abrupt departure, and he put his arm around my shoulders to steady me as I leaned on the rail to get a picture.

Almost immediately afterwards, the leading destroyer made a signal, in obedience to which the third in line broke off and steamed right alongside us in order to establish our identity, and I cursed myself for having been in such an infernal hurry to use that last exposure. When my Father saw I was making no move to seize this opportunity he exclaimed: 'Wake up Boy, now is your chance' and, upon realizing I had no more film, uttered a most heart-felt 'Damn!' which was completely in tune with my own feelings.

During the whole of that day he seemed to be in a state of suppressed excitement and he borrowed a pair of binoculars from the Captain which he kept slung round his neck for the rest of the voyage. As we steamed up the English Channel, through the Straits of Dover and the Thames Estuary to Tilbury Docks, there was plenty of Naval activity to engage his attention – and mine – but those three destroyers, at times almost hidden by the spray as they drove through the heavy seas, were to him, something very special – maybe a symbol of the sea which he loved and the Service which he so greatly admired – never at any other time do I remember him displaying greater emotion than he did on this occasion.

Chapter Seven

AFTER SPENDING a few days in London we returned to Capel House where we received an exuberant welcome from Hadji and a more staid but equally affectionate one from Mother's maid. The rest of the domestic staff had departed to do war work or, in the case of the chauffeur, into the army. Mother was able to secure the services of two young girls, who had just left school, to help in the house but no attempt was made to replace the chauffeur. Many of my Father's friends had been caught up in the war machine in one way or another; Gibbon was in Russia as a War Correspondent, Curle joined the R.N.V.R. and Walpole was chained to some Government Department in London.

My Father decided to buy a second-hand Model T. Ford the controls of which were similar to the old Cadillac, so that he felt he could drive and look after it himself when I was not around.

My own immediate future was very much under consideration at this time, and eventually it was decided that I should go to a Tutor at Oxford and renew my studies with a view to making another attempt to get into Sheffield University. I departed to join the tutorial establishment of the Reverend Long with some reluctance. I was feeling very unsettled, the pursuit of learning held no attraction, and the news that my friend Conrad Hope had joined the Royal Flying Corps, increased my feeling of unrest.

However, the 'Long' establishment was quite bearable and my two fellow-students proved to be pleasant companions. Long was an enthusiastic oarsman and soon organized us into a 'four', stroked by himself, and the daily spell on the river made our studies far more pleasant. It also provided us with some amusement owing to the fact that the reverend gentleman wore a wig – approximately the same colour and texture as Hadji's coat – which slipped forward over his eyes as he rowed. He would clutch at it hurriedly from time to time in an endeavour to restore it to its proper position, with the result that it was often back to front by the time we disembarked – a fact of which he seemed completely unaware – so that his appearance as we walked back from the river attracted considerable attention.

One Sunday morning, I was taking a stroll along the Banbury Road when I came upon a Ford car which had broken down. Its driver, an Army Warrant Officer, appeared to be unable to put the trouble right, so I offered my help which was gratefully accepted. It so happened that I was able to locate the fault at once, and I was thanked profusely and offered a lift back into Oxford which I accepted. During this short journey, I discovered that the Warrant Officer was in charge of a recruiting mission in the city and some further conversation resulted in a decision on my part to enlist at once. I informed my Father by letter and received in reply, a telegram forbidding me to do anything of the kind and telling me to return home at once.

Although I was only just seventeen, J.C. – as my Father was now affectionately called by all of us – made no attempt to dissuade me from volunteering, but he insisted that my period of training in the *Worcester* entitled me to apply for a commission. A few days later he took me to London and we visited the War Office from whence we emerged with a promise that I would be granted a commission in the near future. In celebration of this event, we proceeded to the Café Royal where my health was solemnly drunk in Lager – the choice of beverage, needless to say, being J.C.'s, not mine.

We had gone to London in the Ford and the return journey was marked by an incident which might have ended in disaster. It had been a showery day, and as we passed through Sidcup, the roads were wet and slippery. My high spirits, resulting from the success of our expedition may have induced me to drive too fast for these road conditions and we went into a most spectacular skid, spinning round two or three times and then striking the kerb sideways with great violence. The impact was on my side of the car and caused it to tip over onto its side far enough to throw us both out. As I landed heavily on the pavement, J.C. passed over me in full flight and, while still air-borne, enquired anxiously 'Are you all right, Boy?' I scrambled up to go to his assistance, but he was already sitting up and waved me away saying 'you better run after the damned thing unless you want to walk home'. The car had dropped back onto its four wheels and was rolling gently along the road. I went after it as instructed and by the time I had re-started the engine and backed it to the scene of our mishap, J.C. had picked himself up and was now on the other side of the road, deep in conversation with a young woman who was selling flags – 'Flag days' were prevalent at that time. He bade the lady a most elaborate farewell, sweeping his grey bowler hat – now battered and dirty, from his head and bowing ceremoniously, then he walked across the road to the car, replacing his headgear at a jaunty angle. Having taken his seat and settled himself comfortably my Father handed me one of the flags saying:

'Ram this into your coat', then produced and lit two cigarettes, one of which he passed to me, at the same time indicating that he was now ready to resume the journey.

I was gazetted Second Lieutenant on September 20th, 1915
and within a fortnight I was in uniform and under orders to
report to the Training Centre at Grove Park. J.C. announced
that he would take me there in the car, but when we reached
Bromley he told me to drive to the station where he got out
and shaking me warmly by the hand, told me that he and
Mother – now known as Mrs. C. – had decided that I should
keep the car with me while at the Training Centre and that
he would go home by train.

I was deeply touched by this generous gesture on the part
of my parents in depriving themselves of their sole means of
transport and I was determined to return the car to them at
the earliest possible moment. Accordingly, at the end of my
first week's training, I sought an interview with the Adjutant
and, on the pretext of very urgent family affairs, secured a
twenty-four hour pass which enabled me to take the car back
and spend a few hours at home before returning by train.

Strange as it may seem in these days, my instruction in the
duties of a junior officer in H.M. Forces occupied exactly
four weeks and then I found myself posted to a Siege Artillery
Brigade. After a few weeks on Salisbury Plain we were
ordered to Clarence Barracks, Portsmouth and it seemed very
likely that we would soon be sent overseas. When I wrote to
tell J.C. he replied at once, urging me to try for forty-eight
hours' leave.

I put this suggestion before my Commanding Officer with
whom, owing to certain sins of omission, I was temporarily
far from popular. It was rejected and I was provided with a
job of work in lieu, but luckily this involved going to Wool-

wich in charge of a convoy of lorries to draw stores. Upon our arrival there I immediately handed over to my second-in-command – he was just seven days junior to me in length of service and about ten years my senior in age – appropriated the Sunbeam car in which we had led the expedition, and made a dash for home, only about forty miles away. I arrived in the small hours of the morning and tapped on the study window where a light was still burning. J.C. accepted my unexpected arrival quite calmly but, having asked for an explanation and been told the true facts, screwed his monocle into his eye and treated me to to the most savage glare I ever remember; then, patting me on the shoulder, he said: 'Go up to your Mother for five minutes then come down to me, you must be under way again in an hour.'

When I rejoined him he said: 'Look here, Boy, in case you should get yourself "knocked on the head" out there, I should at least like to know where your remains are disposed of.' He then explained a code he had divised by means of which I could let him know approximately what part of the front I was on, without running foul of the censor. Many years before he had taught me to play chess and he now gave me a pocket chess set and said that we would play games by post. Certain moves, not relating to the games in hand would, when used by me, indicate squares which he had ruled on his war map. Then he escorted me to my car, shook me vigorously by the hand and said: 'Be off now, Boy – Bless you.'

Although very emotional, he kept his feelings rigidly under control on this occasion – which is more than I can say for myself – and I was thankful that he turned and re-entered the house at once, instead of standing to watch my departure.

This was in November 1915 and now, looking back over more than fifty years, I picture him prowling about his room, after my departure in the first light of dawn, puffing savagely at his inevitable cigarette until he had regained his composure sufficiently to return to his desk and concentrate upon the last chapters of the *Shadow Line* – the book which is dedicated to me, and for which I have a very special affection. It is, as he has written, 'an exact autobiography' and was originally intended to bear the title *First Command*.

I have the feeling it still bore this title when we parted and that he decided to change it when he returned to his desk.

In Richard Curle's copy he wrote: 'This story has been in my mind for some years. Originally I used to think of it under the name of *First Command*. When I managed in the second year of War, to concentrate my mind sufficiently to begin working again I turned to this subject as the easiest. But in consequence of my changed mental attitude to it, it became *The Shadow Line*.

There are passages in this book which I can repeat from memory, for instance:

'Only the young have such moments. I don't mean the very young. No. The very young have, properly speaking, no moments. It is the privilege of early youth to live in advance of its days in all the beautiful continuity of hope which knows no pauses and no introspection.

'One closes behind one the little gate of mere boyishness – and enters an enchanted garden. Its very shades glow with promise. Every turn of the path has its seduction, and it isn't because it is an undiscovered country. One knows well enough that all mankind has streamed that way. It is the charm of universal experience from which one expects an uncommon sensation – a bit of one's own. One goes on recognizing the land-marks of the predecessors, excited, amused, taking the hard luck and the good luck together – the kicks and the halfpence, as the saying is – the picturesque common lot that holds so many possibilities for the deserving, or perhaps for the lucky. Yes. One goes on. And the time too goes on – till one perceives ahead a shadow line warning one that the region of early youth, too, must be left behind.

'This is the period of life in which such moments of which I have spoken are likely to come. What moments? Why, the moments of boredom, of weariness, of dissatisfaction. Rash moments. I mean moments when the still young are inclined to commit rash actions such as getting married suddenly or else throwing up a job for no reason.'

For the next two years, contact with the family was confined to my infrequent periods of leave from the Front, except for the news of their welfare and activities derived from the letters which reached me at irregular intervals; sometimes I would hear nothing for several weeks and then receive several letters at once. Mrs. C.'s contained news of J.C.'s health and activities, and of my brother's development and adventures; and J.C.'s provided news of Mrs. C. which was increasingly distressing. During the first year of my absence her knee was getting steadily worse and the pain and difficulty in moving about increased. In fact, it was not until J.C. made the acquaintance of Sir Robert Jones – a famous orthopaedic surgeon in those days – that any real progress was made to alleviate her suffering. Sir Robert became a close friend of my parents and, in a series of operations during and after the War, he succeeded in making Mrs. C.'s condition far more bearable. Unfortunately, he arrived on the scene too late to fully repair the damage done by his predecessors. J.C.'s letters invariably mentioned the great help and comfort that 'the young Scamp' – i.e. brother John – was to them both during this period, and he also indulged in some very frank criticism from time to time of the manner in which the War was being conducted.

In addition to those of his friends who were able to visit him, I gathered that he received visits from people actively engaged in the conduct of the war, and he was also greatly concerned about the ultimate fate of Poland. Joseph Retinger had re-appeared on the scene and was very much involved in this problem, with both the British and French Governments.

It was not, however, until I returned for my first period of leave, in March 1917, that I learned from Mrs. C. and John, of the hazards which many of the war-time visitors to Capel House had to encounter. It seems that J.C. usually made the journey to Ashford Station to meet his guests and that his method of driving the Ford had given rise to some comment. In particular his habit, when suffering from a gouty hand, of leaving the car in the station yard with the engine running while he went onto the platform to greet his visitor, thus sparing himself the pain arising from manipulating the starting handle. Having collected the unsuspecting victim, he invariably hustled him, or her, into the rear seat explaining at the same time that he liked to have plenty of elbow-room when driving. He would then set off at a brisk pace which, however, did not prevent him from carrying on an animated conversation over his shoulder with the occupant of the rear seat. When, as was not infrequently the case,

112

some remark was made with which he disagreed, the vehemence of his reply called for some gesticulation which was hindered, but by no means prevented, by the fact that he was gripping the steering wheel firmly in both hands. The resultant gyrations of the Ford from one side of the road to the other sometimes caused the unfortunate passenger to arrive at our door in a state bordering on collapse.

The letters which he wrote to me while I was in France were always read many times. For me they conveyed an intimate warmth strong enough to give the illusion of his physical presence in whatever hole in the ground I happened to be occupying at the time, and I bitterly regret that I no longer have them. In fact, all but three vanished together with most of my personal belongings when I became a casualty less than a month before the armistice, and these later passed out of my possession as a result of my own folly and I have, as yet, been unable to trace them. The first – in chronological order – reached me in July 1916 when I was involved in the Battle of the Somme. In it he told me at some length about a letter he had received from a man who was serving a fifteen-year sentence in Dannemora Prison, New York. As I have said, I no longer have this letter but I do have a photostatic copy of the letter written to J.C. by the prisoner – Le Roy Ruhl, and also a letter written by J.C. to Mr. Eugene Saxton of Doubleday Page & Co. his publishers and I reproduce them here:

Dannemora, New York, June 4, 1916.

My dear Mr. Conrad,

I am serving fifteen years in Dannemora Prison. The only existence I can live wherein my faculties can have their sustaining exercise is in the pages of a book. I was fortunate enough to get the loan of a copy of *Karain* – decrepit and ravaged from much use – a few weeks ago, and that accounts for my letter. My enjoyment was something beyond my powers of expression.

If there are any battered, tattered, hopelessly unvendible likenesses of this volume – say *Lord Jim, Chance*, etc. – destined for the scrapheap, will you for kindness' sake, have the publishers send them to me?

Sincerely,
Le Roy Ruhl 11356
Box 'B' Dannemora,
N.Y.

J.C.'s reaction was prompt and characteristic:

Mr. Eugene Saxton,
c/o Doubleday Page & Co.,
Garden City,
New York.

4th July, 1916.

Dear Mr. Saxton,

The enclosed explains itself. Will you stand my friend here and arrange for a complete set of the *Deep Sea* limp leather edition to be sent to the unfortunate man from Doubleday Page & Co's offices and debited against me in my account.

I am working as well as I can. My health now seems to have taken a turn for the better; but the strain of the state of war grows no less – on the contrary!

Our kindest regards to Mrs. Saxton and yourself.

Believe me cordially yours –

Joseph Conrad.

P.S. Heard from our boy yesterday; but we hear the guns in Flanders night and day.

The second was in reference to his dedication to me of the *Shadow Line* which reads:

'To 'Borys and all the others who, like himself, have crossed in early youth the shadow line of their generation.'

With Love.

What I remember very clearly from it is that he said he was sure I would understand his reason for including the 'all others' in a dedication originally intended solely for me.

His brief visit to the East Coast at the request of the Admiralty was the main subject of the third letter. In it he explained why he had accepted this assignment, and commended Mrs. C. and John to my care if he should fail to return.

There is no doubt that he greatly enjoyed this adventure, although he said very little about it in later years – even to me. Some odd scraps of information did, however, come from the young naval officers who were involved in it with him. For instance, his stubborn refusal to be parted from his bowler hat when he went for a flight over the North Sea. It seems that he thrust aside all offers of more suitable head-

115

gear for flying in an open cock-pit, but finally agreed to anchor the bowler by passing his silk scarf over it and then tying it under his chin. Nevertheless, when he went on board the 'Q' vessel – H.M.S. *Ready* – for a cruise in search of enemy submarines, he showed no hesitation in discarding the bowler in favour of a dilapidated peaked cap.

Chapter Eight

It was in the spring of 1916 that I first learned of my parents' friendship with Lord Northcliffe and also of the entry into our family life of a lady who remains to this day something of a mystery to me. It may appear in the ensuing pages that I am writing mostly about myself but I believe this is needed to provide some of the background to the picture of our family life during this period, when I was separated from them by the English Channel and pre-occupied with the duties of a junior officer on active service. This letter, written by J.C. to Richard Curle, who was then in Africa, seems to me to provide an explanatory background:

My dear Curle, we were glad to hear from you. We hope you are now settled down and improving in your health rapidly.

Of public affairs I have nothing to say that you don't know already by the cables. Borys wishes in his last letter to be remembered to you. He's still with the guns being now att^d *personally* to the artillery of the III^d corps. I suppose he is as much in the actual scrimmage as an officer of his corps can possibly be.

I will confess to you that I miss you considerably. Your departure, following on Marwood's death, left a great void. Our life here has been running in its usual groove, but I am sorry to say Jessie has not been so well as she is usually. John flourishes and keeps you in mind. Gibbon returned from Russia a week ago and without seeing us proceeded to Switzerland to seek the bosom of his 'petite Famille'. Millais is invalided out of the Navy for good. He and his Mother made friendly enquiries as to your health. We made the acquaintance of a new young woman. She comes from Arizona and (strange to say!) she has an European mind. She is seeking to get herself adopted as our big daughter and is succeeding fairly. To put it shortly she's quite yum-yum. But those matters can't interest a man of your austere character. So I hasten away from these petty frivolities to inform you that we had here Lord Northcliffe for a Sunday afternoon. He was an immense success with John and Robert.[1] In about fifteen minutes they became extremely familiar with him, dragging him all over the place to look at birds' nests and so on. In return for these attentions, he invited them for two days to his house in Broadstairs. They are going there soon in the great man's Rolls-Royce which will come for them. That same subtle Northcliffe got round the Lady Jessie[2] by feeling references to his mother, which certainly had the stamp of sincerity on them . . .

Retinger's activities go on at white heat – personal success immense, political what it can be and indeed better than one would have thought it possible in the hopeless state of the Polish question. He created for himself certain titles to a hearing by accomplishing a brilliant piece of work last month as an unofficial intermediary between the Br. and Fr. Governments. In truth the position was delicate. But its too long a story for this letter. I too have dipped my fingers in diplo-

[1] Son of Norman Douglas.
[2] Mrs. C.

macy by writing a memorandum on the peace settlement on the Eastern front which got into the F.O. The official I interviewed later said as I was leaving – 'Well, I never thought I would have this sort of conversation with the author of *The Nigger of the "Narcissus"*.' Which shows the man to have the sense of contrasts in him, though he looked like a stick of sealing wax and seemed to be made of parchment. For the rest, a perfect *homme du monde* and some years ago (I understand) known for his *success de salon* – of the non-political kind. Well – I must stop now – the continuation in my next.

Affect^te regards from us all.

Yours ever,

J. Conrad.

The news contained in this letter is approximately in chronological order in so far as it impinged upon my movements in France during the next twelve months.

Gibbon came straight from his family in Switzerland to the Western Front as correspondent of the *Daily Chronicle* and his very first act after installing himself in the War Correspondents' H.Q. in Amiens was to locate my unit and pay me a visit. I was, of course, delighted to see Reggie – the courtesy title of Uncle had by now been discarded – and we had much information to exchange. He naturally wanted full details of our journey back from Poland and I was equally anxious to hear about his experiences in Russia and to have news of his wife and daughters in Switzerland. My Commanding Officer was in a sufficiently benevolent mood to release me from duty for a few hours, so I followed Reggie's Press car back to Amiens on my motor-cycle and he introduced me into the War Correspondents' Mess where I was their guest at dinner. Beech-Thomas was the senior correspondent at that time and I have very pleasant memories of my first meeting with him. Reggie refers to this occasion in a letter to J.C. as follows: '... Borys is an ass! he has nothing to be grateful to me for. I have something to be grateful to him for though, and that is the jolly boyish sort of respect he gives me, which always stimulates and refreshes me. I have the biggest kind of liking and belief in that kid. And, by God, hasn't this business made a man of him! You ought to see him by a muddy road-side with his wagons and his sergeant, and his calm competence and appetite, and his infantile bad language, and his little half-conscious swagger when he invites me to come and have a drink. I took him to dinner at the War Correspondents' Mess, and the fellows after first being impressed by his ancestry took to him unanimously – which is a damn sight more than they ever did to me ...'

Clearly Reggie wrote this letter with the object of pleasing J.C. and, no doubt deliberately, omitted any account of the final stages of that party. In fact the hospitality of the War Correspondents' Mess was so lavish that it affected me to a certain extent, and also wrought havoc among a number of my hosts. Therefore, when I had at last succeeded in making it clear that I must return to my duties, I was accompanied down the stairs and out into the street where the cold night air quickly eliminated the majority of my escort. Those few who were still able to stand insisted upon helping Reggie – who, as always on such occasions, seemed perfectly normal – to plant me on the saddle of my motor-cycle, point me in the general direction of the Front Line, and give a good hearty shove. It is said there is a special providence watching over the young and the inebriated – maybe I qualified under both headings, but I prefer to believe I was quite capable of getting back to my unit without the initial assistance of my kind hosts. Reggie and I only managed to achieve one more meeting before he was transferred to the Italian Front to cover the German offensive there.

The Western Front during the summer of 1917 was very quiet so far as the Somme sector was concerned and for a time the Cavalry was dismounted and sent in to man the trenches in front of our gun positions in order to relieve the Infantry battalions. Soon after this change had been carried out I became aware that some officers were getting four-day periods of leave to Paris.

I had received letters from both my parents telling me more about the glamorous lady from Arizona who seemed to have established herself firmly with them. J.C.'s letters to me described her in considerably more detail than Mrs. C.'s and also provided the information that she had now moved on to Paris, and I got the impression that she was mixed up in some way with Joseph Retinger's activities about which J.C. had also written to me. I had not yet met the lady and was most anxious to do so. Her name was Miss Jane Anderson or Mrs. Jane Anderson Taylor, depending apparently on the situation in which she found herself at any given time, and I believe she was actually introduced into our home by Lord Northcliffe, although J.C. did not specifically say so in his letters.

I decided to make a bid for some Paris leave in order to make Jane's acquaintance; also I was very curious about Joseph Retinger's movements. Our Artillery Staff-Captain at that time was Bruce Ingram of the *Illustrated London News* – and it is was through him that I got my first Paris leave. As soon as I knew that my application would be granted I sent a letter to J.C., asking him to write to me at the Hotel Meurice and let me know Jane's Paris address and also to try and get in touch with Joseph (Retinger) and tell him to contact me there.

The leave train got to Paris about six in the evening and I grabbed a cab and went straight to the hotel. There was no sign or word from Joseph so I bathed, discarded breeches and field boots in favour of a pair of slacks, and went straight to the Hotel barber's where I passed an expensive but very satisfying hour availing myself of all the services provided; after which I adjourned to the cocktail bar collecting J.C.'s letter from the reception clerk en route. This informed me that Jane had a suite at the Hotel Crillon. It also contained a further brief summary of the lady's attractions followed by the blunt advice to 'take care not to make a damned fool of yourself'. The effect was to make me more anxious than ever to meet Jane, and I telephoned the Crillon, only to be told that Madame was out and not expected back until ten o'clock. I returned rather disconsolately to the cocktail bar which, by now, was full of senior officers, and immediately got myself involved in a stupid altercation with one of the Assistant Provost Marshals who appeared to think there was something suspicious in the presence of a mere lieutenant in the midst of this exalted company, and asked me for my credentials. These I had to produce but I was in no mood to be pushed around by someone of equal rank, even if he *was* wearing Staff uniform and an Assistant Provost Marshal's band round his arm, and I finally told him to 'Go to hell' and went into the restaurant for dinner. A piece of foolishness on my part which could have proved quite serious.

At ten o'clock I was sitting in the vestibule of the Crillon with my eyes glued on the revolving doors and at about ten-fifteen Jane swept in. I recognized her at once from J.C.'s description; we had supper in her sitting-room and she was able to give me detailed news of my parents and John – she had stayed with them several times. It was she who gave me the details about J.C.'s flight over the North Sea and his cruise in the 'Q' vessel H.M.S. *Ready* and it appeared that she knew Lieutenant Osborne who commanded her and several of the other officers concerned. By the time I got back to my room at the Meurice – at about three a.m. – I realized that I had fallen heavily for Jane.

Joseph and two friends invaded my room in the morning at what I felt – under the circumstances – to be a disgustingly early hour. Joseph insisted I should spend the day with them and also proposed that I should then be escorted around the night spots of Paris. I fell in with their plans for the day but firmly declined the evening proposal – I had a date with Jane for dinner, as soon as she returned from some visit she was making outside Paris. We finished up in Joseph's rooms and, when I prepared to leave at about eight o'clock, Joseph accompanied me down to the street and, as we parted, said: 'I suppose you are going to see Jane?' I admitted that this was so and, from the expression on his face, it was quite clear that he was disappointed that I should abandon him in this manner.

I took her to dine at one of the fashionable restaurants, and quickly discovered that she appeared to be upon friendly terms with most of the clientele, the majority of whom seemed to be high ranking British and French officers. More-over, she was clearly a valued patron of the establishment and somewhat to my embarrassment, we were escorted with great ceremony right across the room, by the *maître d'hôtel*, to what proved to be her favourite table. After the meal, which I would have enjoyed more without the constant inter-ruptions by her friends, I suggested we return to her suite at the Crillon, to which she agreed. We had hardly settled down in Jane's sitting-room and ordered coffee when Joseph's landlady telephoned to say he had been taken ill and wished one, or both, of us to come round. Jane told me that this was not the first call of this kind that she had received. She said that Joseph had been working far too hard and had developed some sort of nervous disorder which affected him from time to time, but that it was not considered serious, and we might as well have our coffee before going to him.

His condition looked alarming enough, to me, and we spent the remainder of the night either holding him down in the bed during fits of hysteria or breaking evil smelling glass capsules under his nose. However Jane seemed to know the routine and said he would be all right in the morning. This proved to be the case and he went to sleep peacefully enough about dawn, so I took Jane back to her hotel and returned – rather reluctantly I fear – to sit with Joseph until he woke up. By noon he seemed fully recovered so I returned to my hotel for a bath and a shave and then collected Jane and we went out to Versailles to visit some friends of hers.

My leave ended the following day and the leave train left Paris at six o'clock in the evening. Jane had engagements all day but promised to try and get back to the Crillon in time for me to have tea with her before leaving. I spent part of the day with Joseph and then went round to the Crillon, taking my kit-bag with me. It was four o'clock – in no time at all it was five o'clock – then five-thirty and still no Jane. I determined to miss the leave train; there was another at midnight which was reserved for senior and staff-officers and I decided to get myself on to it somehow. At six-thirty Jane returned; she looked grave when I explained why I was still there, and said we better dine in her suite because I should keep under cover until I went to the station. In due course I said goodbye to her, took a taxi to the station and boarded the staff train without difficulty. I had scarcely made myself comfortable in a corner seat when my antagonist of the cocktail bar appeared with two of his minions and gleefully informed me that I was under arrest for overstaying my leave. I was escorted to the Provost Marshal's office where the Captain on duty readily granted me permission to make a phone-call. I told Jane of my predicament and she said: 'O.K. I'll have you out of that in no time at all.' She did just that – within an hour I was back in her sitting-room – she certainly had friends in the right places.

The next leave train was, of course, at six o'clock the following evening so Jane managed to get me a room at the Crillon adjoining her suite and I went to bed eventually with the pleasing knowledge that I had another whole day's leave ahead of me. We set out quite early and I suppose I spent one of the happiest days of my life, although I remember nothing of what we did or said.

On this occasion Jane escorted me to the station and saw me on to the train – she was taking no chances.

By the time the train reached Amiens I had arrived at the following conclusions: That I had had a wonderful five days; that Jane was quite unique – in my, then somewhat limited, experience; that I had completely forgotten to ask Joseph about his activities; that I had mortgaged at least two month's pay and allowances; that I still knew nothing about Jane's background and activities. In fact I realized that the only piece of concrete information she had disclosed about herself was that she had once been married to a man called Taylor in the U.S.

I duly reported to my Commanding Officer and explained the reason – up to a point – for my delayed return; to my relief he chose to regard my encounter with the Provost Marshal's people as 'very funny'. As soon as I had an opportunity I wrote to J.C. giving him a full and true account of everything except for Jane's part in getting me released from custody – this had to be omitted at the time in case my letter came under the scrutiny of the Field Censor. I also informed him of the precarious condition of my finances. His reply was prompt and characteristic. First he informed me that he had taken steps to put my finances in order and then expressed the hope that the enemy would keep me sufficiently pre-occupied to enable me to 'get Jane out of my system'. No other comment – I don't think I ever heard him make use of that dreadful phrase, 'I told you so' nor do I remember him indulging in recriminations under any circumstances.

Chapter Nine

WHEN I, at last, got some home leave, at the beginning of 1918, my parents were occupying a furnished flat in Hyde Park Mansions off the Edgeware Road. This was in order that Mrs. C. could be fitted with an extremely heavy and clumsy metal splint with the object of keeping her knee quite rigid. When I arrived she was already encased in this devilish contrivance, and must have been suffering the most acute discomfort although, as always, she gave no visible sign.

I was feeling somewhat guilty because upon disembarking at Southampton, I had allowed myself to become involved with a brother officer in the entertainment of two young ladies and had thus squandered two precious days of my leave. By way of atonement for this unfilial behaviour and in order to afford some distraction for Mrs. C., I invited her to accompany me to the theatre – the invitation was also extended to J.C. but only as a matter of form; there was no chance of him joining in such frivolity. Mrs. C. was delighted at the prospect of seeing a show and we set off happily together. I had already secured gangway seats and we started early enough to enable her to get herself comfortably installed before the rush. After the performance, which she thoroughly enjoyed, we waited till most of the audience had departed before making our slow progress to the exit where I had previously arranged for a taxi to be waiting.

Having got her settled as comfortably as possible, we set

127

out for the flat, but just as we reached the junction of Piccadilly and St. James's Street, there was an air-raid warning. Our driver immediately made a reckless right turn into Dover Street, pulled up at the tube station and made a dive into its depths like a rabbit into its burrow, accompanied by a number of other people. I made a move towards the door with some vague idea of pursuing the man and dragging him back to his cab, but Mrs. C. placed a restraining hand on my arm: 'Don't dear. You will never find him', she said, with that unshakeable placidity which was characteristic of her. I enquired, rather irritably I fear: 'Then what the devil do we do – just sit here?' Her answer came promptly in the usual calm and gentle voice: 'You could drive us home dear!' This simple solution was clearly too good to ignore and I climbed into the driver's seat and urged the elderly Napier taxi in the direction of the flat.

The Edgware Road, as we proceeded along it, appeared completely deserted until I discovered a small dark object approaching down the exact centre of the highway. As we drew nearer together the object became identifiable as an elderly gentleman arrayed in full evening dress, complete with opera hat and open overcoat flapping round his legs as he ran. As we passed one another it became clear the poor fellow was near the point of exhaustion and running with blind determination to reach his goal.

Upon our arrival at the flat, we found J.C. sitting peacefully by the fire reading. He made no mention of the air-raid warning and only interrupted his reading just long enough to enquire, rather casually, whether we had enjoyed the play.

After I had poured drinks for J.C. and myself and made tea for Mrs. C. she recounted our adventure in her gentle voice. My male parent was sufficiently interested to put his book down upon the table and give his undivided attention to the narrative. He then briefly damned the taxi driver and, as he reached for his book, said to me: 'Better telephone the Police or you may find yourself arrested for stealing the cab.'

The following extract from another letter which J.C. wrote to Richard Curle makes it clear that Mrs. C. and I did not confine our outings to a single theatre visit but, strangely enough, I remember only the incident described above.

'... Early this year we spent some time in London on account of Jessie's knee. The surgeon put the limb in splints of a particular kind and assigned a three months' period to observe the result of that truly infernal-looking implement. It brought instant relief; and though the beastly affair weighed nearly six pounds she managed to go about a good deal with Borys who was on leave just then. These two racketted together for a fortnight, dined in a club with Mrs. Wedgewood, who was charming to them both, visited theatres undeterred by the numerous air-raids and generally had a good time. I had gout. The B. returned to France to be involved in the 3rd Army's mess and we went back to Capel to await developments. It was a horribly trying time...'

I do, however, remember very clearly an incident which occurred on the evening of the last day of my leave. J.C. had invited a former Battery Commander of mine to dine with us at Verrey's Restaurant in Regent Street – which he frequently used when entertaining his friends in London. Colonel James Lithgow, who had been a Territorial Major when in command of our Battery, was wounded during the Somme battles and awarded the Military Cross. In civil life he was the head of a famous ship-builders on the Clyde and, after recovering from his wounds was withdrawn from active service and given the post of Director of Merchant Ship Production – for which he later received a Knighthood.

Owing to Mrs. C.'s difficulty in walking, I took her straight into the Restaurant and installed her at our reserved table, then returned to the vestibule where J.C. was waiting to receive our guest. Colonel Lithgow arrived at that moment and we all went to the cloakroom for J.C. and the Colonel to deposit their hats and coats. I had already disposed of mine before taking Mrs. C. to her seat, so that I was in a position to give my full attention to what followed. J.C. with his usual courtesy, relieved the Colonel of his cap and 'British Warm' and turned away to deposit them, and his own hat and coat with the attendant, leaving our guest talking to me. There were a number of people waiting at the counter among whom was a large and resplendent person positively dripping with gold braid and medals, who had his arm outstretched in readiness to take his coat from the attendant. J.C. who disliked waiting about in these circumstances and was, moreover, anxious to rejoin our guest, apparently mistook this lavishly decorated being for the commissionaire, and seized upon what he imagined to be an unexpected opportunity of ridding himself of his burden. He therefore flung the Colonel's British Warm over the gold encrusted outstretched arm followed smartly by his own overcoat; then added his bowler hat and the Colonel's cap as he turned away saying: 'Bring the ticket to me in the Restaurant.' The victim of this outrage remained motionless – whether from astonishment or indignation was not yet clear. Fortunately our guest was talking to me and saw nothing of all this so, as J.C. rejoined us, I made some hasty excuse and went forward to try and retrieve the situation while J.C. escorted Colonel Lithgow into the Restaurant. To his great credit I found the

American Naval Officer convulsed with laughter, and I thankfully relieved him of his unexpected burden and escorted him to the cocktail bar for a restorative.

When we returned to the flat Mrs. C., who was in great pain, retired at once to her room and I settled down by the fire with J.C. for a long talk.

I was due to return to France the following morning and it was obvious that my impending departure was weighing heavily upon him. For all his professed optimism, I sensed that he realized, just as well as I, that the metal splint in which Mrs. C.'s leg had been encased was simply to immobilize the limb for a period, in the hope that the inflammation would subside somewhat before another operation. Mrs. C. remained, as always, outwardly calm and unruffled and I am sure that any anxiety she may have felt was not as to the outcome of the operation, but solely concerned with the probable effect upon J.C.'s health.

When I left next morning my parting from her was as unemotional as ever – so far as she was concerned. As I bent over to kiss her she patted me on the arm and said: 'Run along dear!' One would have thought I was merely going for a walk in the park. I blundered out of the room only to have the remnants of my own composure shattered by J.C. who embraced me with emotion instead of giving me the usual slap on the shoulder and firm handclasp. I think this was one of the unhappiest moments of my life.

The news from home during the ensuing weeks grew progressively worse and then ceased abruptly when I became submerged in the German offensive of March 21st.

When we eventually came to the surface and began to receive our mail again, Mrs. C.'s next operation had already been decided upon, but about this time our battery was withdrawn for a rest and this news must have been a great relief to my parents. J.C. mentions it in a letter which he wrote to his great friend Sir Sydney Colvin, the text of which is given here:

22/4/18.

My dear Colvin,

Pardon this scrap of paper. I have been at it all day and I haven't the energy at this hour (11.30 p.m.) to go downstairs and get a whole sheet.

And truly I wouldn't have enough news to cover it. We had letters from B. dated up to the 20th inst. His battery have been sent back for a rest (the first time this happens to him since he went to France) and he writes the letter of the 20th from some town (either Rouen or Havre I guess)[1] seventy miles still further back, where he and some other officers had run for a day or two to get clothes and some provisions. I reckon those boys must have lost all their kit in that infernal *bagarre*. But the battery is safe and the kid is unhurt so far. He's a good child. He remembered hearing me say once that I liked a special kind of olives, saw some in a shop and is sending me a jar of them – out of the very jaws of death as it were. I feel horribly unworthy.

The work progresses – such as it is. I hope you are getting better in earnest. I may have to run up to town for a few hours on Thursday. Great nuisance. Pray give my love to Lady Colvin and forgive me this empty chatter.

Ever affectionately yours

Conrad.

[1] He was wrong – it was Boulogne.

The work mentioned in this letter was probably *The Arrow of Gold* or it might have been *The Rescue* which he had put aside twenty years earlier and resumed again about this period – 1916/17 – on the advice of his agent J. B. Pinker.

When the date for the operation was fixed I applied for ten days' compassionate leave, which, I am thankful to say, was granted. My young brother was also brought home from school so that the whole family were there at the time.

In due course I returned to my battery and my brother returned to school leaving J.C. in solitary attendance upon Mrs. C. until she was sufficiently recovered to return home. He refers to this in another letter to Richard Curle as follows: '... the bones have grown together, I am told; and considering that the joint has been in a horrible condition for upwards of fourteen years a slight set back after the operation was not to be wondered at. Yesterday she has actually put foot to the ground and walked a few steps in her room in the nursing home. This is the first time in more than three months. The present disposition of the family forces is as follows: Mr. and Mrs. J. Conrad are going to retreat to Capel House next week according to plan. Lieutenant B. Conrad is advancing in Flanders with the Second Army and is much bucked. Master John Conrad is interned in a preparatory school in Surrey for his third term and is now reconciled to his horrible situation ...'

This letter was dated October 9th, 1918 and only one day later my own good luck deserted me when I became partially buried, with several others, by a salvo of high explosive shells among which the enemy had included several gas shells. The effects of the gas and my temporary interment put an abrupt end to my participation in the War and remained with me for several years. In fact, in a minor degree, they remain with me to this day.

Eventually I found myself at No. 8 Red Cross Hospital, Rouen, and wrote from there a brief note to J.C. It so happened that, owing to some delay in reporting the casualties on that occasion, the official War Office telegram had not, as yet, reached my parents, so that my brief letter was their first intimation that I had become a casualty. The result was that when the official telegram eventually reached them about a week later they, not unnaturally, jumped to the conclusion that I had recovered, returned to my unit, and been wounded again. This caused them great anxiety until they received another letter from me.

Again he wrote at once to Sir Sydney Colvin about me and this letter is actually dated three weeks before the Armistice.

> Capel House,
> Orlestone,
> Nr. Ashford.
> (October, 1918).

My dear Colvin,

B. has been sent after all to base hospital (N. 8 Rx) which I guess is in Boulogne.[1] He was with his battery major at the time and they were both much bruised with lumps of earth and flying stones. He describes himself as perfectly right while in bed but feeling shaky when he gets up. He regrets being away from his column at this exciting time, but has no idea how long they are going to keep him in the hospital. He talks of his enormous appetite and is obviously pleased

---

[1] Wrong again. This time it *was* Rouen.

to have plenty to eat. Methinks our Flanders army has been advancing on a light diet.

Our dear love to Lady Colvin and yourself.

Yours ever,

Conrad.

Chapter Ten

AFTER THREE or four weeks in the Rouen Hospital I seemed to be fully recovered physically, but my nervous system was in a very bad state and I was transferred to a 'shell shock' hospital – officially called a Neurological Hospital – in South London which did me no good at all. Although it was a military hospital commanded by a Colonel of the Royal Army Medical Corps, the discipline was very lax and those of us who were physically mobile received virtually no treatment. There was a 'games room' and a billiard room where we spent most of our time, and, as we were allowed to play cards, it was not very long before the 'games room' became nothing more than a gambling den! We became increasingly bored and discontented, but this state of affairs was temporarily alleviated by the fact that the Night Nurse was persuaded to allow some of us to leave the hospital at night and roam around the neighbourhood. Before long these nocturnal activities developed into nightly excursions by underground to the West End where we frequented the bars, and made a general nuisance of ourselves. Fortunately for all of us these excursions were brought to an abrupt end by one of the party who, while returning by the last train from Piccadilly Circus, became suddenly convinced that the carriage was a German dug-out and decided to 'mop it up' single handed. He embarked upon this enterprise with enthusiasm – having first armed himself with an umbrella snatched from an inoffensive passenger, which he used as a substitute for rifle and bayonet. Fortunately the rest of the party were able to overcome him before any serious damage was inflicted, but the railway authorities sent for the police who provided an escort back to the hospital. Although I had been on one or two of these excursions, I was not in the party on this occasion – for which I was very thankful. Obviously there was going to be trouble both for the patients and hospital staff and I therefore decided to write to J.C. and tell him the facts. He did not answer my letter but – characteristically – took some immediate action, which resulted in my being summoned to the office of the Commandant and informed that I was to be granted three months' sick leave at the request of my parents who wished me to be under the care of their own doctor. I was delighted to be home once more and very relieved to be out of that unpleasant establishment before the inevitable official enquiry got under way.

I have no direct knowledge of the outcome of this, but I believe that it received a certain amount of attention from the Press.

The first thing I heard from my parents when I returned home was that we had to leave Capel House, which distressed me very much. Our friend and landlord, Mr. Edmund Oliver, had died some months earlier, and his son and heir decided that he wanted to live at Capel House himself and therefore had given notice terminating our tenancy.

We were all very sorry at having to leave Capel; of the homes we occupied from the time of my parents' marriage to the day of J.C.'s death, it held the happiest memories, in spite of the war. That pile of mellow bricks and weathered tiles, though not beautiful from an architectural point of

view, seemed to me to possess an atmosphere of warm friend-
liness and permanence. I believe our parents had the same
affection for the place as my brother and I had – and still
have. We lived there for nearly nine years; longer than in
any of our other homes except Pent Farm. Efforts to find a
suitable dwelling in the area had, so far, proved unsuccessful
and time was running out, not only because our new landlord was pressing for possession of Capel but also due to the
fact that Mrs. C. was facing the prospect of yet another major
operation and was most anxious to get the family settled
somewhere first. The situation was also made more difficult
because J.C. was determined to remain within this area of
Kent which we had all come to regard as our native habitat.
Finally it was decided that we should seek some sort of temporary accommodation until an acceptable dwelling became
available. This was promptly and unexpectedly provided by
Captain Halsey, R.N., who very kindly offered us the furnished tenancy for six months of his mansion in the village
of Wye – between Ashford and Canterbury.

Spring Grove was a much larger house than Capel and
therefore we were able to provide accommodation for our
domestic staff, some of whom had attended upon a daily basis
at Capel owing to lack of space. It is appropriate to state here
that my parents were invariably accorded the utmost loyalty
and devotion by their employees, and the very infrequent
changes were regarded as a calamity.

In due course the main part of our household furniture
was put in store in Ashford, and our personal effects, essential
equipment, domestic staff and my dog Hadji were transported from Capel to Spring Grove – a distance of approximately nine miles.

Hadji, who by now was beginning to feel the burden of

139

the passing years, had always been a very tolerant animal. Tolerant that is to say in respect of the odd and unlikely pets which my brother John acquired from time to time.

There were, for instance, some wild ducks which my brother had hatched out – with the aid of a hen needless to say – and kept upon the remnants of the moat which had once encircled Capel House. Also, there were of course the cats' recurrent litters of kittens, all of which, including the ducks – would congregate outside the kitchen door at feeding time, and through the middle of which Hadji would delicately pick his way, wearing an expression of – in more or less equal parts – long suffering resignation, contempt and disgust. This is not so improbable as it appears – he had an exceptionally expressive physiognomy.

I remember only one occasion when his patience and tolerance temporarily failed him. This was when, owing to some marital indiscretions among the feline population, there were even more kittens than usual. Hadji was observed industriously digging a considerable hole among the potatoes; having completed this operation to his satisfaction he proceeded – with the utmost care and gentleness – to remove the kittens, one by one, and deposit them in the communal grave he had already prepared. So far as I remember he was in the actual process of depositing his fourth victim when the operation was abruptly brought to an end by the intervention of my brother.

This digression is for the sole purpose of offering some justification for Hadji's behaviour upon our arrival at Spring Grove. As is usual when renting a furnished house, we were presented with an inventory of its contents – in duplicate – one copy of which had to be signed and returned to the owner. Unfortunately an item had been omitted from this document – viz. one household cat – female and, as we very soon discovered, pregnant.

Hadji was the first to make this discovery and his violent reaction was, in my view, perfectly justified. After all, tolerant acceptance of cats belonging to a loved 'young master' was just one of the burdens of a dog's life, but this was beyond canine endurance, and he therefore chased the unfortunate animal round and round the house until it finally eluded him by climbing a creeper which grew up the wall, and sought sanctuary upon the flat roof. Thereupon Hadji instituted a blockade which was so effective that we were compelled to pass food and milk through the skylight in order to save the prisoner from starvation.

All this may appear to be somewhat irrelevant but it had an exciting and amusing sequence as will appear later.

We soon made ourselves at home at Spring Grove, and although little or nothing has been written about this period in J.C.'s family life – probably owing to the brevity of our tenancy – there were, nevertheless, several happenings which I think are worthy of mention.

We went into residence in the early spring of 1919 and *The Rescue* was finished during the first weeks of our tenancy. J.C. wrote to Richard Curle on May 25th, 1919 as follows:

My dear Curle,

I've just finished *The Rescue*. My poor wife has to contemplate the delightful prospect of another operation in about three months time.

I've here a set of privately printed booklets (of various things of mine) for you, also a first edition of *Shadow Line* and a complete set corrected proofs of the new edition of *Nostromo*. All that may prove to you that you have not been forgotten.

Au revoir then. Drop us a line.

Yours always,

J. Conrad.

J.C. began both *Suspense* and the dramatization of *The Secret Agent* at Spring Grove and here too he wrote jointly with J. B. Pinker, a film script of *Gaspar Ruiz* under the title of *The Strong Man*.

The house seemed always to be full of guests among whom Curle, Walpole, Gibbon and Jean Aubrey seemed the most frequent. Also a friend of my own, a former brother officer, now demobilized and who, having a wealthy father and therefore no pressing cares or anxieties as to his own future, had adopted a somewhat exaggerated *laissez–faire* attitude towards life in general which seemed to cause J.C. some amusement. Ralph Pinker – younger son of J.C.'s literary agent – was a student at Wye Agricultural College which was situated near at hand and he also contrived to spend a fair amount of his time with us.

Mrs. C. was again so crippled that she was virtually house-bound and the urgent search for a new home was carried out by J.C. and myself. The old T. Type Ford had been traded in, at Mr. Hayward's rapidly expanding establishment, for a Studebaker open four seater. It was the most modern car we had as yet owned, and had a high standard of performance for that period. Until we secured the services of a chauffeur – which was not for some months – I did all the driving and maintenance, which I greatly enjoyed. In fact driving J.C.

around and enjoying the companionship of those who were continually coming and going at that time did me far more good than the ministrations of our family doctor.

Upon our house hunting expeditions the spare seats in the car were usually occupied by any guests who happened to be staying with us at the time, and it was on one of these occasions, when Walpole was with us that he incurred J.C.'s displeasure by commenting upon the speed at which I was driving.

It was during our tenancy of Spring Grove that an American lady and her daughter became frequent visitors. I have no knowledge of the circumstances under which they came to be included among our circle of friends and I think the first contact must have been made when I was in hospital or, possibly, still in France. Mrs. Grace Willard – she was a widow – and her daughter Catherine, then about seventeen were very charming, but I have never been able to understand why they were upon such intimate terms with my parents, Catherine always called her mother 'Mama Grace' and it was not long before she was so addressed by all of us; I regarded her daughter as a welcome addition to the younger element among those who came and went at that time – she was a good tennis player for one thing.

There was a period when I strongly suspected that Mrs. C. was fostering some matrimonial ideas about Catherine and myself – possibly she thought marriage would accelerate my recovery – but no such idea entered my head at that time. Although she was a good looking girl – handsome rather than pretty – and had an excellent figure, she was a 'big girl' in every sense of the word, and large females have never held any attraction for me.

Mama Grace seemed to occupy most of her time in searching out various pieces of antique furniture, also old silver and cut glass, most of which she succeeded in selling to J.C. – he had a strain of the collector in him – and I am pretty certain that Mama Grace's income depended to a considerable extent upon these transactions. It is, however, only fair to say that everything she succeeded in 'unloading' upon him was genuine and in good condition. As to whether the prices she charged were reasonable or not I have no knowledge.

The sequel to the rigid sentence of exile imposed by Hadji upon the Spring Grove cat developed at breakfast time on a fine morning – by the way, I had forgotten to mention that, some weeks earlier, the cat had been 'blessed with issue' to the number of five and that their knowledge of the world and its dangers had been hitherto confined to about six square yards of flat roof. So far as I can remember there were present that morning at table: J.C., Walpole, Gibbon, Jean Aubrey, my ex-army friend, Mama Grace and Catherine. Mrs. C. had not, as yet, put in an appearance but I believe my young brother arrived on the scene at the last moment as it were.

J.C. who liked to enjoy a leisurely breakfast on those occasions when he had a group of his friends around him, took his seat at the head of the table, and told our young parlour-maid to 'open a couple of those windows, and bring in the coffee and my letters'. The girl duly carried out her instructions and retired from the room to continue her daily duties which included, at this hour, feeding the cats on the roof; but on this occasion she forgot to close the skylight again!

The dining-room at Spring Grove was large and had tall windows at one end and along one side which were suitably draped with thick curtains. As the meal drew to its close

144

cigarettes were being lit and J.C. was in the act of opening his letters when a most horrifying din assaulted our ears. Before we could even begin to speculate as to the cause of this pandemonium all the cats rushed into the room hotly pursued by Hadji, Dora the parlourmaid, and her young sister from the kitchen quarters. Hadji and the girls were all in full cry as they made several circuits of the breakfast table at top speed. Then four of the kittens sought safety by climbing up the curtains – from where they were later removed with some difficulty – the fifth leapt through the window and vanished for ever; the old cat also withdrew, back to the roof, as we discovered later, and spurned all our efforts to induce her to abandon this refuge. For all I know to the contrary her skeleton remains there to this day.

During the whole course of the engagement J.C. remained seated at the table opening his mail and making no contribution other than to flap his table napkin irritably at the cats as they zoomed past and issuing a general directive to: 'Get these damned animals out of here.'

Having finished with his correspondence he said: 'Go get the car, Boy. We are going to London. I have to be at the American Embassy at noon in order to sign some documents!'

It was then nearly ten o'clock and, hitherto, my best time for the journey to London stood at one hour fifty minutes. Clearly I had a considerable challenge on my hands. I ran for the car and when I brought it to the door J.C. was already waiting, attired as usual in havelock and grey bowler hat. Walpole who had intended to return to London by train on that day was also waiting, having decided – misguidedly as it proved – to travel with us. My army friend, who sensed the possibility of some excitement made the fourth member of

145

the party, sitting by my side, while Walpole and J.C. occupied the rear seat.

The car was going perfectly and we made excellent time on the open road but when reaching the London area south of the Thames the traffic became very dense. In those days about half of it consisted of horse-drawn vehicles, mostly delivery wagons and heavy brewer's drays each drawn by a pair of huge cart-horses. This sort of slow-moving traffic was a great hindrance when one was short of time; but I pressed on – maybe rather recklessly – and eventually pulled up outside the U.S. Embassy.

When I turned in my seat to look back at J.C. he already had his big old-fashioned silver watch in his hand, attached as always to his person by a heavy gold chain. He opened it, then turned its face towards me and said: 'Well done, Boy.' It was exactly ten minutes to twelve and I had trimmed nearly eight minutes off my previous record time!

It was not until J.C. had got out of the car that I realized he was bare-headed, and asked him: 'Where is your hat?' He gave a casual shrug of the shoulders and answered: 'Oh! I guess somewhere in the gutters of Camberwell.' Then as he turned to enter the Embassy he added: 'Better take Hugh home then come back here and wait for me.' Before carrying out these instructions I turned again in my seat with the intention of seeking fuller information regarding J.C.'s missing head gear. I have often heard and read of people described as being 'green with fright' but this is the only time in my life that I have been privileged to see anyone suffering from this interesting condition. Hugh was sitting rigid and motionless, with hands clasped tightly in his lap, and eyes very wide open, staring fixedly ahead. His usual florid complexion had paled, and there was an unmistakable tinge of

146

green in it. He took not the slightest notice when I spoke to him, so I drove on to No. 99 Piccadilly where he shared a first floor flat, overlooking St. James's Park, with a friend.

Although he had revived somewhat by then, he was still speechless and we had to assist him out of the car and into the entrance where we dumped him in the lift and told the porter to deliver him to the care of his friend.

We then drove round the corner to a well-known bar in Shepherd Market for an aperitif before returning to the Embassy. J.C. emerged just as we drew up and indicating with a gesture, that my friend should remove himself to the rear seat, settled down by my side and announced his wish to be driven to Scott's – the famous hat-shop. In due course he emerged from this establishment and came towards the car swinging his walking stick in a jaunty manner and wearing a pleased expression and a lustrous new grey bowler hat adjusted at the somewhat rakish angle which he was prone to favour when feeling in a particularly happy mood. He informed us that he was hungry so, by mutual agreement, we proceeded to The Royal Automobile Club in Pall Mall, of which we were, all three, members. It was a most excellent and well-equipped club in those days and J.C. invariably used it as his base when in London on business. During the meal I asked for fuller details regarding the loss of his hat and was informed that 'It was knocked from my head by the nose of a gigantic dray-horse when you cut across its "bows".' I then asked him whether he thought this incident had contributed to the pitiable condition to which Walpole appeared to have been reduced? He gave one of his abrupt shouts of laughter and said: 'No doubt. He is a dear fellow but so damnably timid at times.' In this I think J.C. was a little unfair to Hugh – had I been a back-seat passenger on that journey

147

I have no doubt my feelings would have been very similar to his. As for J.C. himself, he had a blind faith in my ability as a driver, which was quite unjustified in the light of my relatively limited experience at that time. Now, with more than half a century of driving behind me, I am appalled by the contemplation of the risks to which I exposed my parents and myself in those early days.

After a leisurely meal my friend decided to remain in London for a couple of days before rejoining us at Spring Grove, and departed, while J.C. and I headed for home – making a call at Mr. Hayward's garage in Ashford en route. We had been aware, for some time, that Mrs. C.'s apparent reluctance to come for a drive in the Studebaker was due to the fact that she was quite unable to make herself comfortable in it, owing to the rather cramped seating accommodation, and the object of our visit was to ask Mr. Hayward to try and find us a larger car. A few days later he appeared on our doorstep with a 30 h.p. four-cylinder Cadillac for Mrs. C. to try. She found it quite comfortable both in the front and rear seats and was delighted at the prospect of being able to sit by my side again. A bargain was made at once with Mr. Hayward and, a few days later Catherine and I took the Studebaker into Ashford and collected the Cadillac.

The sudden hurried journey to the U.S. Embassy was in connection with the sale of film options on some of J.C.'s books – for which he received over £3000. It seems that the agreements had to be signed at the Embassy.

I believe it was upon the first occasion that I took both my parents for a drive in the Cadillac that we discovered 'Oswalds' – the house in which J.C. ended his days. Mrs. C. and I fell in love with it at first sight, but J.C.'s reaction was more restrained – not in so far as the house was concerned, which he agreed was pleasing in appearance, adequate in accommodation, had a bowling green, three mature and beautiful walled gardens with communicating doors between them, a large garage with living rooms above for a chauffeur, and an electric generating plant! His sole objection was that the house, and the village of Bishopsbourne, are at the bottom of a deep fold in the downs. He complained that there was no view. I replied that we had no view from the Pent or from Capel House. He retorted that we could at least see more than one hundred yards. I pointed out that within ten minutes by car he could be on top of the North Downs from where he could see the Thames Estuary. Finally he decided that the obvious advantages outweighed his sole objection, and negotiations with the owner – Col. Bell – began the following day. I am convinced that he was as happy during those last years of his life as his own failing health and Mrs. C.'s continual suffering permitted. That his objection to 'living in a hole' must have persisted is, however, borne out by a letter he wrote to Richard Curle on October 1st, 1922, in a postscript to which he states clearly that he has given his landlord twelve months' notice. The letter reads as follows:

Oswalds,
Bishopsbourne,
Kent.
1st October, 1922.

Dearest Dick,

I can't let the new month begin without asking how you are. In truth all at once I have become quite anxious about you. Do please drop us a line; a comprehensive line to tell us shortly of your 'public' and 'private' activities.

Are you going to invest in the Dy. Mail stock?

How is your health,

(a) physical

(b) mental

(c) moral – by which I mean the degree of depression or exaltation from which you may suffer.

We thought you may (might) have proposed yourself for this weekend. Lady Millais came to lunch on Friday and asked about you.

I have been doing nothing but thinking – absorbing myself in constant meditation – over the novel.[1] It's almost there. Almost to be grasped. Almost ready to flow over on the paper – but not quite yet. I am fighting off depression. A word from you would help. Our love.

Ever yours,

J. Conrad.

P.S. I've given a year's notice to Bell!! Am scared now.

I heard nothing directly of this from Mrs. C., but I was rather out of touch with them at that time, having been sent up to Manchester to take charge of the Daimler Co.'s newly opened Sales Office there.

Presumably he must have withdrawn his notice or perhaps Col. Bell – with whom he was on terms of friendship – had not taken the matter seriously. This is pure speculation, but it is a fact that, during the last six months of his life he was looking for another home.

[1] *Suspense* – which he never finished.

Chapter Eleven

THE MOVE to Oswalds took place in August 1919: *The Arrow of Gold* was published during the same month and during the rest of the year J.C. was mainly pre-occupied with completing the dramatization of *The Secret Agent*, the first three acts of which were finished before he took Mrs. C. up to Liverpool for yet another operation at Sir Robert Jones' own private nursing home. J.C. himself stayed at 85 Kingsley Road, Liverpool. There was a railway strike at the time that the move was carried out, with the result that all forms of road transport were at a premium, and there was no immediate hope of getting our furniture transported from storage in Ashford to our new home. Moreover the transportation from Spring Grove of our personal belongings, J.C.'s books, Mrs. C.'s invalid chair and numerous other items, seemed to present some difficulty, but I was able to borrow a dilapidated motor lorry and to enlist sufficient voluntary labour to solve this problem. Mrs. C. was at this time awaiting the expected operation which Sir Robert Jones had insisted should take place in his own private nursing home in Liverpool on December 2nd.

In a letter to Curle dated October 15th, 1919 J.C. says: '. . . We are camped here with a few sticks of furniture, without curtains or carpets and, in our horrible state of suspense, not caring to undertake anything more.'

This gloomy assessment of the situation did not, however,

take into consideration Mrs. C.'s indomitable spirit, and by November 22nd – the eve of her departure to Liverpool for the operation – she had supervised the domestic staff to such good purpose that Oswalds already had the appearance of having been occupied for some time, and when she returned from her ordeal she at once resumed the direction of the household from her bedroom.

The accommodation on the ground floor included an entrance hall with a long passage leading to the rear of the house giving access to a very large room which had recently been added as a billiard room. This she decided to make into a formal drawing-room, thus enabling her to retain a smaller room for use as a 'den', such as we had at Capel, to which she could retire and rest on her long chair and which my brother and I could share with her when we were at home. The large dining-room and J.C.'s study were situated on either side of the front door and opened onto the entrance hall

There was no suitable furniture available for the big drawing-room, and it was as a result of this deficiency that Mama Grace came to be involved again. In fact she provided everything necessary – curtains, pictures, couch, chairs, Aubusson rugs for the parquet floor and even a baby grand piano. How much money she extracted from J.C. for all this I have no idea, but it must have been a considerable sum. Again, in justice to Mama Grace, I must stress that the result, as I remember it, was very pleasing.

The large kitchen was at the end of another passage leading off at right angles; into the length of which two doors had been fitted – for no apparent reason. As a result of this, there existed, between J.C.'s study and the kitchen – where Mrs. C. was usually to be found when sufficiently mobile –

152

no less than four doors, and I well remember an occasion upon which I was talking to her, as she prepared our lunch when J.C. entered abruptly and demanded to know what had become of a certain letter which he had received that morning. It was subsequently located in the pocket of the dressing-gown he was wearing. Upon being told by Mrs. C. in her usual quiet way, that she had last seen it in his hand, he threw out his arms in a wild gesture and retreated to his study, slamming each of the four doors violently en route. Mrs. C. who was supporting herself upon her crutches and had a huge frying pan in her hand, remained motionless waiting patiently for the slam of the fourth door and then turned placidly back to the kitchen range without comment.

About this time I was summoned before a Medical Board and invalided from H.M. Forces as permanently unfit for active service; I was also granted a disability pension of £150 per annum. The question of a career for me now arose and J.C. enlisted the help of some of his friends to try and find an opening for me with an engineering firm, but there were many other young men of my age with no specific qualifications also looking for jobs, so that no immediate prospects presented themselves. Meantime I looked after the car and the electric generating plant and drove J.C. around as required.

We had gone about so much together that I had come to know instinctively whether he wanted me to drive fast or slowly and, in particular, when he wanted to light a cigarette. The Cadillac, like all its predecessors, was an open car, so that the lighting of his cigarette required a degree of co-operation from me which I was expected to provide unasked. Owing to the chronic gout from which he suffered, his fingers were usually so swollen that he had difficulty in cupping his hands so as to shelter the flame of a match, and moreover he often wore mittens – knitted for him by Mrs. C. – which were apt to catch fire before the cigarette! He had, therefore, evolved a method which seemed to work perfectly provided I slowed down sufficiently at the right time. He would first place the cigarette between his lips and then extract four matches from the box and arrange them side by side with the heads in echelon. He then struck the first head on the box which in turn ignited the second, and so on, thus creating a progressive conflagration lasting long enough to enable him to apply it to the end of his cigarette. When he sat in front it was a simple matter for me to co-operate, but when he was sharing the back seat with a friend I had to take a hurried glance over my shoulder occasionally to see if he needed a smoke. On one occasion his back seat companion was J. B. Pinker and, assuming they would be absorbed in conversation, I had neglected my duties until reminded by a faint 'Damn' and 'Blast' which just reached my ears before being borne away by the wind. I slowed down at once and looked back over my shoulder just in time to see J.C. hurl overboard his matches, the packet of cigarettes and the unlighted cigarette from his mouth, in the order named. Pinker, who possessed a highly developed sense of humour of a certain kind, assumed an expression of alarm and held on to his hat with both hands in the pretence that he expected it to follow the other articles over the side. This performance earned him a savage glare from J.C. followed a moment later – as so often happened – by a shout of laughter. I regarded this as a suitable moment to hand over my own cigarettes and matches which were accepted and made use of without comment.

It was very soon after we had settled in at Oswalds that I had an experience which affected me very much at the time and certainly retarded my very slow return to normal health. Our landlord, Colonel Bell, whose estate included a considerable acreage of pasture and woodland, had invited me to join him for a day's shooting. It was an informal invitation and there were just the two of us with our respective dogs, and carrying, in addition to our guns and ammunition, a packet of sandwiches and a flask. We spent a leisurely and enjoyable day but had very little to show for it – in fact, when we turned towards home my game bag contained one hare and an elderly cock pheasant, while the Colonel had, so far as I remember, a couple of rabbits and a brace of partridge. Hadji did however try to make his contribution by producing proudly the decayed carcass of an unidentifiable rodent which had clearly died of old age sometime previously; he seemed bitterly disappointed at our refusal to accept it. It was dusk when we separated; the Colonel following a lane which led to the stables behind the Hall while Hadji and I took the foot-path across the fields. When we had covered about half the distance to Oswalds and were in the middle of a particularly large field, I was suddenly overcome by a sensation of exposure to great danger; I felt naked, defenceless and terrified, but eventually succeeded in pulling myself together sufficiently to stagger on to the boundary of the field where I sat down under the shelter of the hedge. I have no idea how long I remained crouching there in a state of semi-consciousness before I was aroused by Hadji licking my face assiduously. His ministrations contributed considerably to my revival and I was soon able to get up and continue on my way. By the time I reached home I felt quite recovered and, in view of Mrs. C.'s state of health and J.C.'s anxiety about her, I decided to say nothing about my experience. Nor did I tell our doctor, but for a different reason – I disliked him intensely and had no faith in him. By acting in this way I, no doubt, made matters worse and for some weeks I had a dread of being alone and a great reluctance to cross a road or any open space unaccompanied. Luckily for me, when I had to go to London to investigate a possibility of employment, I had the good fortune to meet, quite by accident, a doctor who had been our Brigade Medical Officer during the last months of my service in France. I told him of my recent experience and asked him to take me in hand. This he agreed to do and, as he was familiar with the basic cause of my condition, it was not long before I became much better. When I at last succeeded in finding a business opening in London I took a service flat in the same street as the doctor's home and surgery, and for some time I must have been a confounded nuisance in continually going to him – more for reassurance than treatment – but his patience, kindness and understanding never faltered, and I am deeply indebted to him. The 'business opening', which was of brief duration, was called the Surrey Scientific Apparatus Co. It was founded by a friend of Gibbon who had as partner a quite brilliant young radio engineer. Too brilliant in fact, in as much as he defected to a much larger organization – now very well known – with the result that the Surrey Scientific Apparatus Co. expired, engulfing in its death throes, my war gratuity – amounting to £400 and a further £200 provided by J.C. which he could ill afford. The only notable achievement in its brief life was the design and manufacture of equipment with which we attempted to give what must have been the first radio commentary on a sporting event, viz. the Oxford and Cambridge Boat Race. I still have the press photograph taken while I was testing out this equipment.

It was while I was associated with this disastrous enterprise that my parents decided to spend part of the winter in Corsica and the details of this trip are covered by a further letter to Curle reading, in part, as follows:

'My very dear Dick,
Your letter was just in time to catch us before our departure to Corsica.
John has been deposited at Tonbridge (school) and I do hope will be happy there. We are leaving with the car to-morrow at 8.30 for Calais, Amiens, Moulins, Valence, Marseilles, Ajaccio, and the weather is by no means promising.
Borys will take us to Rouen, making a detour from Amiens to Albert to see a little of the Somme front. At Rouen he will leave us and go back to Mortlake where he has a berth with a Wireless Appliance Company.... Jessie trots about with one crutch quite smartly. The only worry is a persistent pain area which we can't get rid of yet...'

Pinker and his wife joined the party in Corsica and the film scenario of *Gaspar Ruiz* was continued; also the *Rover*.
Shortly before this expedition was undertaken I had found an excellent chauffeur for my parents. He had had ample experience both in driving and maintenance, having been previously employed by a near neighbour of ours, Count Louis Zobrowski, a very wealthy young man and a famous racing driver of those days, particularly notorious for his exploits at Brooklands Race Track with a car assembled in his own workshop known as the 'Chitty Bang Bang'. His death in one of the Continental road races was deeply regretted by all racing enthusiasts of the day. The recently acquired chauf-

feur, Vinten, took my parents, and Mrs. C.'s trained nurse, on to Corsica after I left them at Rouen. He eventually married the nurse and I suspect that the seeds of this romance germinated during the visit.

They were both devoted to my parents and remained in their service until after J.C.'s death.

I spent a couple of days in Paris on my return journey, but found very little to remind me of the rather hectic leave period there during the war.

By the time my parents returned from Corsica I was once more looking for employment and, although I retained my service flat in London, I spent a good deal of time at Oswalds.

My general health was now much improved, although I still had an occasional recurrence of the previous experience, and I was desperately anxious to obtain employment, preferably in the Motor Car Industry, so I decided to start at the highest level by offering my services to Messrs. Rolls Royce Ltd., the Daimler Co., and Messrs. D. Napier & Son, and duly despatched a letter to each of them. J.C. was pessimistic as to my chances of getting any favourable replies – he still hoped to find me an opening with the help of one or two of his friends – but he agreed that my approach to these firms could do no harm, and when, some weeks later, I received a letter from the Daimler Co., inviting me to come to Coventry for an interview, he was delighted.

Meanwhile I was happy to spend most of the time at home with my parents. J.C. and I went about a good deal together, and Mrs. C. – who was enjoying an all too brief period of freedom from pain – found the front seat of the Cadillac so comfortable that she was able to make some quite long journeys, even an occasional trip to London to see Lady Colvin.

All our friends were anxious to see Oswalds and there was

much social activity at this time. J.C. was an excellent host and he greatly enjoyed giving Sunday luncheon parties, at which he was always in great form. Intimate friends were invited for the weekend within the limits of the accommodation available, and others travelled from London to Canterbury on Sunday morning by train and were met at the station by our car. There would sometimes be eight or ten guests at the luncheon table, some of them Polish or French, and I was always fascinated by J.C.'s ability to carry on a brilliant conversation in three languages without interfering with his enjoyment of the meal, and still find time to 'damn' his man-servant – who acted as butler on these occasions – for some real or imagined defect in the service. Angela and Carola Zagorska, J.C.'s cousins and nearest Polish relatives, spent a good deal of time at Oswalds during this period and were often present at these Sunday luncheons. Yes, J.C. really enjoyed entertaining his friends and they were equally happy in his company. In Curle's words: 'The position of host at the head of his table before a large and kindred gathering, and the position of a friend in a tête-à-tête conversation late at night in front of a dwindling fire saw Conrad at his best.'

Pinker was also very much in evidence at this time. Occasionally J.C. would go and stay for a day or two with him at his home near Reigate, but more often he was our guest at Oswalds. He was as enthusiastic about horses as we were about motor cars and kept up a large stable. He was a first-class 'whip' and drove a tandem and also a 'four-in-hand'. On one occasion when he stayed with us, he drove over with his 'coach and four'. One team of horses was sent ahead to Wrotham – an approximate half-way point where stabling was available – and I took J.C. to the Pinker home in the Cadillac so that he could join the expedition, which was an

159

unqualified success. It was Canterbury Cricket Week and Pinker decided to take a party of us to the ground by coach. Just as we turned into the entrance gates, Frank Woolley – a famous cricketer of that time – had just completed a century, and the resultant cheering and blowing of motor car horns in acknowledgement of this achievement frightened the horses, in consequence of which we made a rapid and spectacular circuit of the Cricket Ground before Pinker was able to get them under control. The spectators greatly appreciated the additional entertainment thus involuntarily provided.

At J.C.'s suggestion another expedition was undertaken with the coach, to Deal, a town on the Kent coast which he liked, and to which he sometimes took Mrs. C. to stay for a few days. At that time it was mainly concerned with fishing and had not yet become a popular holiday resort. I was not in the party on this occasion, so I missed the excitement when J.C. decided to act as pilot, and directed Pinker through the back streets of the town, with the result that they turned, at full trot, into a cul-de-sac ending in a solid brick wall, against which the leading pair of horses narrowly escaped dashing their brains out.

1 Borys Conrad with his Mother at Pent Farm, 1900.

2 Borys Conrad at Montpelier, 1905.

3 *Top left:* G. F. W. Hope, Joseph Conrad's oldest English friend. *Top right:* John Galsworthy, a photograph taken by H. G. Wells. *Bottom:* Henry James by J. S. Sargent, 1913. (National Portrait Gallery, London.)

4 *Top:* Pent Farm. *Bottom:* Embarking on the first long motor trip to visit the Hopes: Joseph Conrad, Conrad Hope, Borys and, partly concealed, Mrs. Conrad.

5 *Top left:* Reginal Percival Gibbon. *Top right:* Joseph Conrad with his son John in Poland, 1914. *Bottom:* Borys with Edmund Oliver and Joseph Conrad on joining *HMS Worcester*, 1911.

6 *Top:* Borys Conrad with his mother, Poland, 1914. *Bottom:* The study at Capel, Joseph Conrad, his wife and son John.

7 *Top:* Mrs. Conrad and Jane Anderson Taylor, 1916. *Bottom:* Joseph Conrad, his son John and Jane Anderson Taylor, 1916.

8 *Top:* 'Q' ship *HMS Ready*, 1916. *Bottom:* Someries with Escamillo in the foreground, 1908.

Top left: Borys Conrad, 1918. *Top right:* Borys Conrad outside the house in
acow where his father and grandfather had lived. *Bottom:* Springrove.

4 July 1?

Dear Mr Saxton.

The enclosed explains itself. Will you stand my friend here and arrange for a complete set of "~~Deep-Sea~~" to be sent to the unfortunate writer from Messrs D P a Co offices and debited against me in my account.

I am working on well as I can. My health now seems to have taken a turn for the better; but the strain of the state of war grows, no less — on the contrary!

Our kindest regards to Mrs Saxton and ~~yourself~~

Believe me Cordially Yours

Joseph Conrad.

PS Heard from our boy yesterday; but hear the guns in Flanders night and d

10 Letter from Joseph Conrad to Eugene Saxton, New York. (See page 114.)

11 *Top:* Joseph Conrad, an etching by Muirhead Bone at the time of his visit to America. *Bottom left:* Hugh Walpole. *Bottom right:* R. B. Cunninghame Grahame.

12 *Top left:* J. B. Pinker and Joseph Conrad at Pinker's home near Reigate, 1922. *Top right:* Capel House. *Bottom left:* Oswalds. *Bottom right:* Joseph Conrad's study at Oswalds.

Chapter Twelve

I HAD nearly given up hope of any favourable result from my interview with the Daimler Co., when I received a letter from them offering me employment on terms far more satisfactory than I had dared to hope. They also enclosed a list of addresses in Coventry where I might be able to secure lodgings, and I was asked to telegraph my reply and confirm my readiness to report at the factory on the following Monday.

J.C. was, of course delighted, and also as surprised as I was at the salary offered; £400 a year was far above my expectations in view of the fact that I had no qualifications to speak of and no previous experience. As I had only five days in which to make my arrangements, it was agreed that I should go to Coventry at once to secure lodgings and then return to London, give up the tenancy of my flat and bring all my possessions back to Oswalds.

I had no difficulty in securing lodgings and therefore telegraphed to J.C. that I was on my way back to London. When I arrived at the flat I found Vinten waiting for me with the car; so I packed all my possessions into it, handed the keys to the caretaker and set out for home.

During the two days remaining before embarking upon my career, I spent most of the time with J.C., and it was only then that I fully realized the degree of his anxiety about my future. He confessed to me that he had enlisted the help of

Richard Curle to contact as many of the big Midland engineering firms as possible on my behalf – which he was able to
do through his family connections in industry – and, moreover, had authorized him to say that I would accept a purely
nominal salary during training or apprenticeship. J.C. had
also arranged with his agent (Eric Pinker)[1] to provide me
with an allowance for as long as might be necessary. I was
very glad that there was now no need for him to shoulder
this additional financial burden; Mrs. C.'s disability had been
a continuing expense almost from the time of my birth, and
also the kindness and generosity of his nature rendered him
practically defenceless against appeals for help – mostly from
'begging letters' but also, in a few instances, from people
who had become acquainted with him. In fact it was not
until we went to live at Oswalds that he achieved any real
financial security. Among the collection of letters – 'Conrad
to a Friend' – published by Curle, there are many references
to his efforts to get me launched in a career and it is obvious
that he went to a great deal of trouble on my behalf.

I had fully intended, before leaving for Coventry, to tell
my parents that I had married some months previously: that
I shrank from doing so may have been partly due to the reali-
zation of J.C.'s deep concern for my future welfare which
had emerged from our recent talks, and had sharpened my
awareness of the shattering effect which my disclosure would
have upon him; and I left home taking my secret with me.

My departure to Coventry put me out of touch with the
family, but the break did not last so long as might have been
expected. After about five months I was transferred to Manchester to look after the newly opened depot there, and given
a salary increase of £100 per annum – a very considerable

[1] J. B. Pinker had died in the U.S. a year earlier.

rise. Six months later I heard that there was a vacancy at the London depot and that the manager there had asked that I should be appointed as his deputy. This was a totally unexpected piece of good fortune in that it brought me once more within easy reach of the family and incidentally a further salary increase of £50.

It was during the time that I was in Manchester that someone chose to inform Mrs. C. that I was married. It was just before J.C.'s departure to America, and she decided to withhold the news from him until after his return, and wrote me to this effect. She also insisted that I should make no attempt to see him or communicate with him until after she had broken the news. I complied with her wishes, with the result that J.C. was deeply hurt by the fact that I was not present to see him off or welcome him on his return. He was acutely distressed and shocked when told of my marriage which he, at first, refused to believe, but within a few days of my return to London I had a letter from Mrs. C. asking me to come and see them as soon as possible and to bring my wife with me.

Characteristically, he uttered no reproaches when we met, nor did he do so at any time during his life, and he greeted my wife with his usual elaborate courtesy, putting her at ease immediately. The close relationship which had always existed between us, although severely tested, withstood the strain but it was the birth of his grandson which finally restored the old intimacy. Mrs. C. also ran true to form but her greeting was far more reserved and it was several years after J.C.'s death before our relationship again became normal. Her rigid self-control and composure had, I believe, been strengthened throughout the years by her painful disability and her unremitting care and devotion to her husband. She

163

was at this time, again in constant pain and seemed well on the way towards yet another major operation and J.C. was clearly suffering physically from the strain of his American visit in addition to the shock of my marriage and his renewed anxiety about Mrs. C.

I returned to London feeling very worried about both my parents and resolved to pay them another visit at the earliest opportunity, but we were very busy for the next two or three weeks, and also I was having great difficulty in finding a permanent home in London.

The Daimler Co., were the first motor car manufacturers to hold the Royal Warrant as suppliers of motor cars to H.M. The King and members of the Royal family. The current cars had been in use since 1910 and instructions had recently been given to supply new ones. Three cars were involved; two State limousines for the King and Queen and one slightly smaller one for the King's brother H.R.H. The Duke of Connaught. These were now ready for delivery and the ceremony took place a couple of weeks after my brief visit to the family. Incidentally it may be of interest to mention that the new cars had to undergo a most thorough and critical inspection by King George V and Queen Mary before being accepted! The old ones were brought in to our showroom for re-sale to the general public on two conditions: (1) That the Royal Coat of Arms be entirely removed from the door panels and (2) The names of any prospective purchasers be first submitted to the Lord Chamberlain for formal Royal approval. As soon as I saw the car returned from the Duke of Connaught I realized it would be ideal for my parents. It was, of course, in perfect condition and the amount of work it had done, in terms of mileage, was practically negligible. Moreover the bodywork – specially built by Messrs. Hoopers who had been Royal Carriage builders in Victorian times was of superb workmanship and also provided wide doors and extra head-room for the convenience of the passengers when wearing ceremonial robes and head-dress; a feature which, I felt sure would be of great benefit so far as Mrs. C. was concerned. I obtained permission to take this car down to show my parents at the following week-end. They both approved of it and I had no great difficulty in convincing them that it was high time they gave up using an open car, and acquired one which afforded adequate protection from the weather; any lingering doubts they may have had were swept away when Mrs. C. found that she could get in and out of it unaided. They both seemed to be in good spirits once more and I returned to London, feeling much happier, to complete the details of the purchase which J.C. had left in my hands.

My son Philip was born on January 11th, 1924 and a few days later my parents came up to London to see him. I was unable to be present at the introduction owing to pressure of work, but I managed to join them for lunch at their hotel and found J.C. in a great state of excitement and even Mrs. C.'s placidity was showing one or two cracks – they were both obviously delighted with their grandson. He wrote a brief note to Curle after this visit which reads as follows:

Hotel Curzon,
Curzon Street,
Mayfair,
London W.

Dearest Dick,

Sir Robert appointed tomorrow, Thursday 10.30 for his visit to Jessie.

We have been to see B's home and child. The baby is really quite nice.[1] Everything looks quite satisfactory there. Saw B. for a moment about 1 o'clock. He is happy no doubt and looks less strained than ever I have seen him look for the past four years. I hope you'll 'phone me a message early in the morning. After Sir R.J. has been my time is yours. Will you lunch?

Yours ever,

J.C.

I was able to get a few days' holiday early in June which was spent at Oswalds, and J.C. passed a lot of his time talking to his grandson and entertaining him by swinging his monocle on its cord for the baby's entertainment.

Had he lived long enough to see his grandson emerge from babyhood they would have soon become boon companions.

He could communicate with children – even the very young. He was completely sincere with them and knew how to draw them out, so that they talked to him freely, without restraint or self-consciousness.

About mid-July Mrs. C. entered a Canterbury nursing home for yet another operation, and the news regarding J.C.'s health became increasingly unfavourable so, on August 2nd I took my family down to Oswalds for the weekend; arriving there at about seven o'clock in the evening. J.C.'s bedroom was immediately above the front porch and, as soon as he heard my car pull up, he rang his bell and demanded that his grandson be brought to him at once. He lay in his

[1] Conrad took real pleasure in his grandchild. He insisted on the baby being brought to him when he was dying. [Footnote by Richard Curle]

166

bed propped up by pillows with the inevitable cigarette smouldering between his fingers. Although obviously very ill, he seemed quite calm and relaxed and greeted us cheerfully; then indicated with a gesture that the baby should be put upon the foot of his bed immediately in front of him. After about ten minutes Philip was taken through the communicating door into the next room where his grandmother was lying helpless, having been brought back from the nursing home only a few days before, and J.C. begged me to hurry over my supper and come back to sit with him.

We talked far into the night; about my future with the Daimler Company and in particular, about his grandson. We talked also of the past; of Pent Farm, and of our early motoring adventures, and the close and intimate relationship which had always existed between us now seemed closer than ever before. When I left him he took my hand and said: 'Good night, Boy' – then added: 'You know I am *really* ill this time.'

He died early on the following morning. Apparently he had got out of bed and was sitting in the armchair from which Mrs. C. heard him fall. She rang her bell, but when his man-servant reached the room he was already dead.

Hindhead, Surrey   January 8th, 1968.

Epilogue

'I TRUSTED to the fresh receptivity of these young beings in whom, unless heredity is an empty word, there should have been a fibre which would answer to the sight, to the atmosphere, to the memories of that corner of the earth where my own boyhood had received its earliest independent impressions.'

(Poland Revisited – J.C.)

J.C. was right – heredity is not an empty word, certainly insofar as this 'no longer young' being is concerned. In my case it has become stronger with the passing of the years and, since his death, the urge to repeat the journey we all made together in 1914 has grown steadily. However, during the earlier part of my working life such an expedition was not to be seriously contemplated and then the Second World War put an end to the project altogether for some years. In fact I doubt if it would ever have revived to the point of achievement in 1967 without the generous and cordial invitation I received, from the Polish Writers' Union, to visit Poland as their guest.

I was, at first, somewhat daunted by the realizaton that this would now be a lone expedition – a poignant contrast to the 'tribal' visit of 1914 – but fortunately, a close family friend of thirty years' standing, was able to accompany me.

There was no question of retracing the route taken on that previous visit. The tempo of our lives has accelerated so much since then that it would have been an act of nostalgic absurdity to do so and moreover, recollections of Cracow and Zakopane, which had remained dormant for so many years, now emerged with such unexpected clarity that I was impatient to test their accuracy.

We flew from London and as usual, I became quite deaf as soon as we took off so – conversation being out of the question – I passed the time in speculation as to the probable course of events after we touched down at Warsaw; we had made no plans, and all the arrangements for our stay had been undertaken by our hosts.

The warmth and cordiality of our welcome, the care for our comfort, and the trouble which had clearly been taken to ensure that we should see as much of Poland as possible during the time available, proved to be far beyond the scope of my imagination; moreover the high regard in which my Father is held by his fellow-countrymen was a revelation to me. This was an unforgettable visit and, although I very much hope to make others in the near future, it will remain supreme in my memory.

There was a brief incident before meeting our hosts which, although amusing in retrospect, affected me rather differently at the time. Upon disembarking from the plane all the passengers were requested to line up on the runway and an extremely pretty Polish air hostess stood on the gangway and began calling someone.

As I recovered my hearing I heard the name 'Pan Korzeniowski', but it made no impact upon me whatsoever until

I received a painful jab in the ribs from my companion's elbow as she said: 'They are calling *you*'! I stepped forward feeling ashamed and embarrassed at having failed to recognize my own family name, only to be seized and thrust out onto a vast expanse of runway where I was left standing, brief-case in one hand and raincoat trailing on the ground, feeling like an ancient scarecrow which had been abandoned there long ago, by the country-folk as they retreated before an avalanche of concrete in which it had become embedded; my demoralization was completed when I realized that a Press photographer was taking pictures of me.

Fortunately the ordeal was a brief one, and I was rescued by my companion and led towards the Airport Buildings in the wake of the other passengers.

As we stood at the end of the line waiting at the passport barrier I noticed a group of people beyond it, one of whom looked straight at me and raised a hand in greeting. I bear a strong physical resemblance to J.C. which was commented upon many times during the visit, but this recognition from a distance, by someone then a total stranger, gave me great pleasure and contributed considerably to my recovery from the embarrassment out there on the runway.

Throughout my life I have regretted my inability to speak my Father's native tongue and I became particularly conscious of this handicap now that I was about to meet my hosts. I need not have worried – even this difficulty had been foreseen and provided for – and I was introduced to a lady who had been appointed by them to act as my interpreter and cicerone.

Her efficiency in both capacities and her untiring care and devotion to my interests ensured the complete success of my visit. Moreover she, like my companion, spends her life in

171

the field of education, and they thus shared a mutual interest which quickly formed a bond between them: they also, as I quickly discovered, possessed the same inexhaustible energy and vitality against which, having long ago made the discovery that I prefer to tread the pathway of my life at a leisurely speed rather than at full gallop, I determined to be upon my guard. In this I acted wisely, particularly upon an occasion when we visited a lake up in the Tatra Mountains and they conceived the absurd idea that we should take a brisk walk round its perimeter! I sat down on the nearest rock and firmly declined to take any part in their expedition. I lit a cigarette and contemplated the view – which was quite magnificent – while they set out, but eventually I began to feel that there was something lacking – a cushion to insert between me and the rock! They returned in about two hours, still full of energy, and I rose stiffly from my seat to greet them.

When we reached the hotel reporters and photographers were already assembling, and I greatly appreciated the sterling qualities of my cicerone, not only as an efficient and sympathetic interpreter, but also for the manner in which she took command of the situation and prevented me from being engulfed by those who wanted to interview me. There were more press visits the following day and, on our excursions about the city we were usually accompanied by one or more reporters or photographers, but they were invariably so courteous and discreet that I soon ceased to be aware of their presence. I was shown as much as could be crammed into the time at our disposal, even places where visitors are not usually admitted, and in the National Library I was shown many documents and letters relating to my family.

We did not go to Warsaw during our 1914 visit but, had

172

we done so, I am convinced that the re-construction of the city, after almost total demolition, has been carried out with such perfection that it would have seemed as familiar to me as Cracow proved to be when we arrived there. The drive into that city from the airport felt to me more like a return home after a few years absence than a deliberate expedition back through more than fifty years of my life. Everything seemed so familiar; the people working in the fields, the cows grazing by the roadside with their patient attendants standing or sitting near them and in particular, the long narrow horse-drawn wagons. In regard to the latter, however, I was conscious of some difference which I was, at first, unable to identify – it was, of course, the fact that they are now equipped with old lorry wheels and tyres, but it was not until we passed one which still had the old iron-shod wooden wheels, that I realized the change.

Our arrival at the modern Hotal Cracovia temporarily interrupted my growing sense of familiarity with my surroundings but, as soon as we had registered and deposited our luggage, I was asked what I would like to do? 'Go at once to the railway station.' This very definite request was, I suspect, a shock to the members of the Polish Writers' Union in Cracow who had greeted us at the airport – possibly they thought I had been overcome by a sudden desire to return home? In fact, as I explained to them, I hoped that by starting from the station, I should be able to retrace the route into the city which we took in 1914. This enterprise was, broadly speaking, successful in that it brought me at once into surroundings which were completely familiar, although a little confused by the deviations imposed by the 'one-way traffic'. My primary object was to locate the Hotel where we had stayed, the name of which I had completely forgotten. I was unable to identify the exterior, but at the third attempt, we entered one which I recognized immediately, and I walked without hesitation through the vestibule, up the broad flight of steps and turned to the right into that familiar dining-room, apparently unchanged through more than half a century, and pointed out to my companions the table in the far corner at which we were seated when J.C. and his old school-friend confronted one another across the length of the room. I believe that I could have marked the exact spot on the carpet − it looked like the same one − certainly it was the same colour − where they met and embraced. Later we walked in the Square, passed beneath the towers of St. Mary's Church and strolled along the Line A-B, before returning to our hotel. During the ensuing days I was able to re-visit the University where, as I remember, J.C. and I were talking to the Librarian during the last few hours of peace, the school which he first attended, and the street in which he lived with my grandfather.

J.C.'s account of our 1914 visit, contains the following passage:

'That afternoon I went to the University taking my eldest son with me. The attention of that young Englishman was mainly attracted by some relics of Copernicus in a glass case.'

I believe it would have pleased him greatly had he known how deeply every detail of that visit became engraved upon my memory − so much so that, on this occasion, I was quite shocked at finding the Globe no longer in the place where I knew it to have stood, and asked at once: 'Where is the Globe?' When told it had merely been moved to another position I was conscious of a distinct feeling of relief at having the accuracy of my memory vindicated.

During the whole of our visit J.C.'s image was constantly

with me, but never more vividly than upon the evening of our arrival as we walked along the Line A-B.

Arrangements had been made for us to spend a few days in Zakopane and, at the last moment, I decided that I would like to make the journey by road. A car was immediately provided and we set out quite early in the morning. Soon after we got out into the open country our driver pulled up at the road side and made a brief speech which, being interpreted, proved to be an invitation to visit his home and family, a short distance from the main highway. We gladly accepted and were driven, at high speed, for about a kilometre along a rough track and, having first made the acquaintance of his dog and been shown his garden, we were taken into the house to meet his family. His wife was completely unperturbed by this totally unexpected intrusion into her home by three strangers – two of whom spoke only in a foreign language – and gave us a warm welcome; we were given coffee, introduced to her two young children, who rose and greeted us with the utmost courtesy and were shown every part of the premises before continuing our journey, bearing an enormous bag of apples as a parting gift. We were very glad indeed at being afforded this intimate glimpse of rural family life in Poland.

We continued on our way, and, soon after arriving at the hotel, I was approached by a lady whom I immediately recognized as an old and very dear friend who had accompanied us on our previous visit and at whose country home we were to have stayed. I had not seen or heard from her since I bade her farewell in Zakopane when we set out on the hazardous journey back to England in November 1914, and it was an emotional meeting for both of us – the more so in my case, because I had no idea that she was still living.

175

During our brief stay we were able to make some excursions up into the mountains, among them the visit to the lake already referred to, and to locate the house where we stayed in 1914 – unchanged in appearance, but now the administrative offices of a Sanatorium.

While in Zakopane I received the news that this book had been accepted for publication in Poland and, therefore, decided to return at once to Cracow in order to retrace the final stages of the former visit more thoroughly than I had yet done.

We had intended to travel directly to Warsaw by a night train and my cicerone had already booked the sleeping compartments so, instead of cancelling these, we decided to travel to Cracow by motor-coach and join the train there, thus enabling us to spend another forty-eight hours in that city.

During the afternoon of our last day a severe thunderstorm developed over the mountains and continued throughout the evening. My escort having, for once, temporarily deserted me, I went up to my room to read through the translations of all the Press notices about my arrival and subsequent movements, provided by my interpreter who must have sacrificed many hours of sleep in order to carry out the task – she certainly had no opportunity during the days. Later, as I stood at the open window watching the lightning playing over the peaks, my thoughts drifted back through the years to the eve of my former departure – it was snowing heavily then – and I thought of the cold and snowbound veranda onto which I had crept to bid farewell to someone whose name seems indeed, to be the only thing which has become completely erased from my memory – or has it? – at this precise moment a name has flashed into my mind – Sasha? Could this or something very similar, have been the christian name of the

176

girl I parted from out there in the snow? If so, then I believe the chain of memory is now complete.

As I looked down from my window, I realized that night had fallen, and the lights were clearly reflected on the black surface of the flooded street; my attention was attracted by the appearance round the corner of the hotel of one of those little carriages so familiar to my eyes – in fact it could, quite conceivably, have been the actual vehicle in which my brother and I had once ridden with J.C. – so packed with passengers that it was impossible to count them from above. As it passed beneath my window, I noticed the driver busily winding the brake-handle (rather like the handle of a coffee grinder) in preparation for the steep descent which began a few yards farther on. Simultaneously I became aware that the final section of the operating mechanism had become detached from the brakes and was trailing on the road. The driver continued to wind his handle, unaware of the futility of the operation, as the equipage passed over the brow of the slope, and I leaned further out of my window in an endeavour to see how long the horse would tolerate the sudden and steadily increasing pressure upon its hindquarters, before breaking into a gallop in an attempt to escape from it. However, my friends chose this moment to burst into the room clamouring loudly for the evening meal, so that my curiosity remains unsatisfied.

In continuing contrast, our journey back to Cracow was made in brilliant sunshine and there was nothing to remind me of that former one through snow-laden darkness.

My old friend with whom I had so unexpectedly been re-united in Zakopane, had promised to join us in Cracow and to accompany me along those last few miles to the old Austro-Russian frontier – where her husband and I had passed an anxious night trying to get her back from Russian territory – and thence on to her former family home where we were to have stayed. Unfortunately she was taken ill soon after we left and was unable even to communicate with us. However there were, as always during this memorable visit, volunteers at hand to guide and assist me – in this case it was the son of J.C.'s friend who did so much to facilitate our escape into Italy in 1914 – who actually interrupted his holiday and abandoned his family in order to return to Cracow and act as my guide on this final stage. We stopped at the obelisk which now marks the former frontier, and walked a short distance to the top of the rise where I stood for some time gazing at the distant ridge along which I had once seen Russian Cavalry patrols passing to and fro in the early light of dawn. Then on to the country mansion at which we were to have been guests – unchanged in appearance I am assured – but now used as a school.

Thus I completed a journey which started at Capel House, Orlestone in the county of Kent, England, fifty-three years earlier almost to the day!

Later we went to the home of J.C.'s old school-friend, just outside Cracow, where we were visiting at the time general mobilization was announced.

The house, which I remembered so well, is outwardly unchanged, although now divided up into quarters for the workers, but as we stood under the wide portico where we once sat with our host looking down the long vista of garden, at the city bathed in the evening sunlight, the change which has been wrought here over the years was a distinct shock to me. No garden – no stables – and the view of the city now obliterated by the paraphernalia of commerce – vast storage or packing sheds at all angles enclosed within high fences. I

178

turned away sadly which, on reflection, was unreasonable in view of the fact that this is the only blemish upon my memories of the past which I encountered during the whole of the visit.

The next morning we had breakfast with my guide of the previous day at his flat where I was shown many things of great interest including letters relating to the negotiations for that journey across the frontier into Italy in which Mr. Penfield, then U.S. Ambassador, was involved. Later that day I was escorted to see the grave of my grandfather before returning to the hotel to prepare for the night journey to Warsaw.

The train was due about midnight, but we left the hotel early and on arrival at the station, made our way to the appropriate platform, followed by a porter with our luggage which he deposited near the bench upon which we were seated, and departed. In due course, the train arrived: it was so packed with people that it seemed impossible for one more person to squeeze in.

The sleeping-coach stopped right opposite to us and, in contrast to the rest of the train, showed no sign of life within. My cicerone immediately rushed forward and made a flying leap at the door handle – she was not tall enough to reach it otherwise – from which she hung suspended in mid-air. This violent assault upon the door produced no result whatever – it was locked – and at this moment, the train began to move backwards, but she refused to relinquish her grip on the handle and continued to hang from it emitting some piercing and indignant shrieks, apparently with the object of attracting the attention of the attendant – a gallant effort which, unfortunately, produced no more result than her attack on the door handle. After travelling backwards for about fifty yards the train came to rest once more and, at this moment the porter re-appeared, picked up our luggage and carried it away with the obvious intention of bestowing it upon another group of passengers who were waiting some distance along the platform. Our 'intrepid leader' at once released the door handle and dropped to the ground in order to dash off in full cry, to rescue our luggage. Eventually she returned triumphant driving the unhappy porter in front of her.

It now became obvious that the departure of the train was imminent so we made a concerted assault on the other door of the sleeping-coach in which the now repentant porter joined with enthusiasm but, just as we reached it, the door opened and the attendant appeared on the threshold, rubbing the sleep out of his eyes. Unfortunately for him, we were unable to arrest our momentum, so that our combined weight – plus that of the luggage, hurled him across the coach and flattened him against the door on the opposite side. At this moment the train started, the porter fell back onto the platform – luckily he had already let go of our luggage – and the attendant, who had now had all the sleep knocked out of him, escorted us to our reserved compartments. My cicerone appeared to be in no way exhausted by her violent activities, but my companion and I were somewhat overcome by the combination of amusement at recent events and anxiety as to whether we could ever succeed in boarding the train. However the excitement was not yet quite over; upon entering my compartment I noticed a door in the bulkhead which I mistakenly assumed would give access to some kind of clothes closet so, having removed my outer garments and arranged them on the clothes hangers thoughtfully provided by the railway authorities, I turned to put them, as I thought, into the clothes closet but, just as I grasped the handle, the train lurched and I was precipitated into the adjoining compartment, to be greeted with loud cries of indignation from my friends who hastily thrust me back into my own quarters and closed the communicating door again. Convinced by now that I had had sufficient excitement for one night, I climbed into my bunk and slept soundly until we arrived in Warsaw.

After breakfast at the hotel we went to the Publishers, where I signed the agreement for publication of my book and also undertook to write this final chapter which is an incomplete and inadequate commentary upon a visit which I regard as the major event in my life.

Later, I had an enjoyable meeting with members of the Maritime Writers' Club before going to visit my principal host, the President of the Polish Writers' Union, at his country home where we were entertained in a gracious book-lined room, surrounded by literary treasures, the contemplation of which made me regret more than ever, my inability to read or speak my Father's native tongue.

The following day – the last before our departure – I was subjected, for the first time in my life, to a television interview. As we went beneath the lights my interviewer handed me a list of questions which he would ask me, but this 'script' somehow was abandoned almost at once, and I feel sure that the interview went on much longer than originally intended. As I came out from under the lights, half blinded and almost overcome by the heat, I was confronted by the blurred outline of a figure which appeared to be proffering me a tray upon which vast sums of money were piled: assuming this to be some sort of hallucination, I tried to walk through it. My inability to do so jerked me back to reality and I became aware of the voice of my interpreter explaining that this tray-full of money was my fee for enduring the ordeal through which I had just passed. Never before in the course of my life do I remember receiving such prompt payment.

My cicerone had invited us to her flat that evening for supper and to meet her husband, a proposal which – having been instrumental in depriving him of his wife for a period of eighteen days – I viewed with some slight trepidation which vanished at the moment of our introduction, and we spent a delightful evening together.

On the following morning we were escorted to the airport by a member of the Polish Writers' Union, my television interviewer of the previous day – who I discovered, had a vast knowledge of J.C.'s earlier sea-life which I would have liked to hear more about – and of course, my cicerone. She seemed, for once, somewhat subdued and I now realize how tired she must have been after her ceaseless activities on my behalf.

We parted outside the Departure Lounge and went out on to the tarmac to board the plane. As it turned onto the runway I could see through the port-hole at my side, that small group of people still waving their farewells and, as the plane gathered speed, I settled back in my seat warmed by the conviction that I had acquired a number of sincere friends during this all too short visit.